MARLBOROUGH

LEADERSHIP ▪ STRATEGY ▪ CONFLICT

ANGUS KONSTAM ▪ ILLUSTRATED BY GRAHAM TURNER

First published in 2010 by Osprey Publishing
Midland House, West Way, Botley, Oxford OX2 0PH, UK
44-02 23rd St, Suite 219, Long Island City, NY 11101, USA

E-mail: info@ospreypublishing.com

ISBN: 978 1 84908 361 4
E-book ISBN: 978 1 84908 362 1

Editorial by Ilios Publishing Ltd, Oxford, UK (www.iliospublishing.com)
Page layout by Myriam Bell Design, France
Index by Mike Parkin
Typeset in Stone Serif and Officina Sans
Maps by The Mapping Specialists Ltd.
Originated by PDQ Media, Bungay, UK
Printed in China through Worldprint Ltd

10 11 12 13 14 10 9 8 7 6 5 4 3 2 1

Dedication

For my grandson Laurence Alexander Turnbull, born 4 December 2009.

Artist's note

Readers may care to note that the original paintings from which the
colour plates in this book were prepared are available for private sale.
All reproduction copyright whatsoever is retained by the Publishers.
All enquiries should be addressed to:

Graham Turner, PO Box 88, Chesham, Buckinghamshire, UK

The Publishers regret that they can enter into no correspondence upon
this matter.

The Woodland Trust

Osprey Publishing are supporting the Woodland Trust, the UK's leading
woodland conservation charity, by funding the dedication of trees.

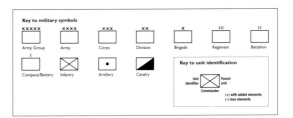

CONTENTS

INTRODUCTION

In the first decade of the 18th century John Churchill, Duke of Marlborough, led an Allied army into battle. His opponents were the French troops of Louis XIV, whose military prowess had made France the superpower of the age. A decade before, a similar Allied army had suffered a string of ignominious defeats at the hands of Louis XIV's French marshals. This time though, there would be no defeat – only a string of spectacular victories. Marlborough's battlefield triumphs at Blenheim (1704), Ramillies (1707), Oudenarde (1708) and Malplaquet (1709) were all the more remarkable because they were won at the head of a polyglot army, with contingents from over two dozen European states, the largest of which were Holland, Britain, Prussia and Denmark. It wasn't just the battles – he also conquered a string of Flemish and French cities through siegecraft, the most spectacular of which was the capture of Lille in 1708. In all respects he was a master of his art.

These great victories were certainly important, but if the Duke of Marlborough was merely a successful military commander then he would

never have achieved what he did. He had to be a diplomat too, constantly pleading with these various states to send him troops and supplies, to reject overtures of peace from France and to agree to fight under a single Allied command. He became the archetypal coalition commander, a man whose skills in diplomacy, language, court etiquette and politics were almost as important as his undeniable genius on the battlefield. The result was that Marlborough almost single-handedly brought Louis XIV's France to its knees – a remarkable achievement for a soldier who had once served the French king as a lowly young captain.

For much of his career, success was a double-edged sword. He gained his first commission through courtly patronage, and subsequent advancements were as much the result of favouritism as martial prowess. He became the friend and confidant of King James II of England and VII of Scotland, who helped move him up the social and military ladder.

Marlborough then betrayed James' trust at the crucial moment. Similarly, the friendship between Queen Anne and Marlborough's wife Sarah meant that he enjoyed a similar trusting relationship with another monarch, which lasted until Sarah and the Queen fell out. Political and military rivals were always jealous of the ease with which the charming, handsome and intelligent officer won the trust and support of these two monarchs. Twice in his career – once under King William and again under Queen Anne – Marlborough was abandoned by his royal patrons, and his enemies took great delight in assisting his fall from grace. On both occasions he survived his downfall, and outlived the monarchs who rejected him to be restored to good grace by their successors.

King James II and VI (r. 1685–88) supported the young John Churchill, but a combination of the King's divisive policies and his religion forced Churchill to switch his allegiance to James' Protestant rival William of Orange. (Stratford Archive)

Today, Marlborough is remembered as Britain's greatest soldier – arguably more successful even than the Duke of Wellington. For six years, from 1704 until 1709, he fought four major battles, and defeated the very best commanders King Louis XIV of France had to offer. For the most part his campaigns were conducted in Flanders, but one of his greatest military achievements came in the summer of 1704 when he outfoxed his French rivals and led his polyglot army deep into Germany. There he succeeded in effectively knocking France's leading German ally – Bavaria – out of the war. This was achieved through two spectacular victories at the Schellenberg and at Blenheim. As a result the military prestige of France was shattered, and Marlborough's military reputation was assured.

Very few military figures lend their name to an age of warfare. Historians talk about the 'Napoleonic' Wars, or the age of Alexander. The Duke of Marlborough is one of few great commanders of history who put such a firm stamp on warfare that their very name became an identifiable era in military history. As the leading military practitioner of the 'Marlburian period', John Churchill, First Duke of Marlborough, was not only the foremost soldier of his generation, but one of the greatest commanders in history. He was certainly worthy of this fulsome accolade.

THE EARLY YEARS

John Churchill may have ended his days living in one of the finest stately homes in England, but he was born into a family that lacked both wealth and status. His father was Winston Churchill, who had backed the wrong side during the English Civil War. Churchill had fought for the King, and as a former Royalist he was viewed with suspicion by the victorious Parliamentarians. When John was born on 5 June 1650, the young Churchill family were living in Ash House – the war-ravaged home of Eleanor, Lady

Drake, Winston's mother-in-law. Lady Eleanor had been a staunch supporter of Parliament, and as her son-in-law had little money, she provided her daughter's family with a home. If relying on the charity of in-laws wasn't bad enough, in 1651 the 31-year-old ex-soldier was fined £480 by the Parliamentarian authorities for 'delinquency' – a legal euphemism for being an unrepentant supporter of the late king.

John Churchill was one of five children, not all of whom survived infancy. We know little of his early childhood, but the fortunes of the family improved after the death of Oliver Cromwell, the Lord Protector, in September 1658. The son of the executed King Charles I returned to Britain in the summer of 1660, and in May 1661 he was proclaimed King Charles II. The joint realms of England and Scotland were kingdoms once more, and the Churchill family enjoyed a swift reversal of fortune. Winston Churchill became a Member of Parliament, a royal administrator, and was knighted in 1664. For his part young John was educated in Dublin, and then St Paul's School in London. His elder sister Arabella became a maid of honour to the Duchess of York, the wife of the King's brother James – the future King James II and VII. Arabella soon become the Duke of York's mistress, and the 15-year-old John became a page in the ducal household.

In September 1667 John Churchill asked his patron for a favour – the gift of a commission in the English Army. It was duly granted, and he became an ensign in Colonel John Russell's Regiment of Foot Guards. The regiment was sent to Tangier in 1668, and young Churchill almost certainly went with them. Tangier on the Barbary Coast of North Africa had been bequeathed to Charles II in a dowry, and it remained a British colony until it was abandoned in 1683. At any rate John Churchill was back in London by 1671, and as a handsome and tanned 21-year-old officer he began to be noticed. As Lord Chesterfield put it, 'His manner was irresistible [to] either man or woman'. John's first known admirer was Barbara Villiers, Lady Castlemaine, a royal mistress and an influential figure in court.

Ensign Churchill became the lover of 'the lewdest as well as the fairest of King Charles' concubines'. Barbara Villiers, of course, was still the King's principal mistress. Court gossip had it that one day the King paid an unexpected visit to Lady Castlemaine's rooms, and Ensign Churchill escaped through the window to avoid a scandal. Another version had the pair caught by the King, who responded by forgiving Churchill, saying: 'Go – you are a rascal, but I forgive you because you do it for your bread.' Soon afterwards, Lady Castlemaine presented her young lover with a gift of £5,000, a present which may have been a reward for his discretion and quick thinking.

Fortunately John Churchill's reputation was saved by a war against the Dutch, and he went to sea on board the Duke of York's flagship HMS *Prince*. He displayed considerable bravery

during the battle of Sole Bay in June 1672, and was rewarded by another commission – this time a captaincy in the Duke of York's (Lord High Admiral's) regiment. He was also removed from the temptations of court by being named part of a small contingent sent to fight alongside the French in their own war against the Dutch Republic. The force was led by the dashing James, Duke of Monmouth, who was the King's first-born but illegitimate son, and the 23-year-old commander of Charles II's army.

In June 1673 the English contingent joined the French Army besieging the Dutch city of Maastricht, and it was there that John Churchill won the admiration of Englishmen and Frenchmen alike. During the final stages of the siege the Dutch launched a night-time sortie and recaptured an important redan. It was there that Count d'Artagnan of the King's Musketeers was killed – a French officer who became the inspiration for Alexandre Dumas' hero in *The Three Musketeers*. The Duke of Monmouth joined d'Artagnan's counter-attack, with Churchill fighting at his side. Eventually the Dutch were repulsed, and the city fell a week later. On their return to court, Monmouth presented Churchill to the King, saying: 'Here is the brave man who saved my life.' It seemed the dashing young officer could do no wrong.

In 1674 he returned to France, and in October led a regiment into action against the Austrians at Enzheim in Bavaria. The French were delighted by his performance – Marshal Turenne praised his military ability, and described him as 'my handsome Englishman'. He returned to court with the honorary title of colonel in the French service; it would be another three years before he received an English commission. It was there that he first saw Sarah Jennings, the headstrong teenage daughter of Frances Jennings, a widowed courtier. By that time Churchill had become the Duke of York's gentleman of the bedchamber, and while Sir Winston Churchill disapproved of the liaison, the Duke and Duchess of York encouraged it, and so, during the winter of 1677–78, the couple wed in secret, probably holding the ceremony in the Duke's London residence.

In February 1678 John Churchill became the colonel of an infantry regiment, and was sent to Holland to open secret negotiations with Prince William of Orange. Colonel Churchill was accompanied by Sidney Godolphin MP, and together they offered the stadholder of the Dutch Republic a diplomatic realignment. Peace between the United Kingdom and the Dutch had been agreed in early 1674. Charles II was now considering a volte-face – allying himself with the Dutch in a new war against the French. Before this, John Churchill had been forging a growing reputation as a soldier. Now he was displaying that he had great diplomatic skills as well. It seems appropriate that the first moves towards an Anglo-Dutch military alliance were proposed by a soldier who would later lead the joint Anglo-Dutch armies into battle.

THE MILITARY LIFE

James' man

In the summer of 1678 it seemed as if England and Scotland would go to war with France. As part of the military preparations – and as a reward for his

John Churchill, Duke of Marlborough, dressed in his court regalia, which is dominated by the necklace carrying the emblem of St George slaying the dragon, the image of the Order of the Bath. Painting by Sir Geoffrey Kneller, c.1702. (Bavarian Schlösserverwaltung, Höchstädt)

recent diplomatic efforts in the Netherlands – John Churchill was made a brigadier of foot, his first real step on the ladder of military command. Weeks later he was back in Holland again, this time at the head of his brigade of five battalions of infantry, which included two battalions of the Foot Guards. It was a prestigious command – the advance guard of an English contingent that was preparing to fight alongside the Dutch. As it happened, the troops never fired a shot. Louis XIV of France made peace with the Dutch, encouraged in part by the prospect of an impending Anglo-Dutch alliance. The resulting Treaty of Nijmegen was signed in August, before Brigadier Churchill could join Prince William's army.

When John returned home he found the country in turmoil. Rumours of a popish plot against the Government led to an explosion of anti-Catholic sentiment. As a Catholic, James, Duke of York, became a target of this, and so King Charles sent his brother to Brussels until the agitation died down. The Churchills accompanied him, but the couple returned to London late in 1679, and while Sarah remained in their house in London – she was expecting their first baby – John travelled to Scotland as the Duke of York's representative. There he helped re-establish James, Duke of York, as a viable successor to his ailing brother, despite his religious handicap. He remained a diplomat for the next two years. The Duke himself visited Scotland, and in early 1682 he was almost drowned when the frigate HMS *Gloucester* foundered off the Norfolk coast. Churchill helped save the Duke by commandeering the only boat and keeping the crew at bay with his sword while James clambered to safety. For this Churchill was rewarded with a Scottish title, becoming Baron Churchill of Aymouth in December 1682.

On John's return to London the young couple continued to live in their own town house in Jermyn Street, but they also bought Holywell House near St Albans, which was Sarah's old family home. Their first child – Harriet – was born in late 1679, but she died soon afterwards. Fortunately other children would follow – Henrietta (1681), Anne (1684), John (1686), Elizabeth (1687) and Mary (1689). Another son – Charles (1690) – died in infancy. Despite this growing family the couple were still needed at court. In 1683 Lady Sarah became the lady of the bedchamber to Princess Anne, the second daughter of the Duke of York, after her marriage to Prince George, brother to the Danish king. The two women – princess and commoner – formed a strong bond, a relationship that would play an important part in the life of Sarah's husband in the years to come.

King Charles II died in February 1685, after a deathbed conversion to Catholicism. John Churchill was dispatched to Versailles to take the news to King Louis IX, and to inform him that Charles' brother James, Duke of York, would accept the throne and become King James II of England and VII of Scotland. Churchill took part in the coronation in late April 1685, and became the King's gentleman of the bedchamber. The following month he received an English title – Baron Churchill of Sandbridge. Then, courtly life was interrupted by news that on 11 June James, Duke of Monmouth, had landed at Lyme Regis in Dorset, and was inciting a Protestant rebellion against the new king.

The Monmouth Rebellion

Within a week of his landing more than 6,000 supporters had rallied to the Duke of Monmouth's cause, by which time Brigadier Lord Churchill was already marching towards the rebels at the head of eight troops of horse and five companies of foot. By 17 June he had reached Bridport, while Monmouth was 20 miles (32km) away, marching on Taunton. Churchill set off in pursuit, but on 19 June he learned that the inexperienced Earl Feversham would have overall command of the Royal army. On 25 June Monmouth abandoned his plans to capture Bristol, and headed south again. The two sides skirmished at Norton St Philip two days later, and Feversham's men were repulsed. Churchill's rearguard of dragoons prevented the rebels from pursuing, and so Monmouth slipped away again to the south and west.

By 3 July Monmouth's army was in Bridgewater, by which time deserters had reduced his numbers considerably. The Royal army of 3,000 men was camped a few kilometres away at Sedgemoor, just outside the village of Westonzoyland. Monmouth decided to launch a night attack – an ambitious venture with experienced troops, and a rash one with an army of 4,000 untrained rebels. Forewarned, the Royal army was deployed for action, its front protected by a deep, black-watered drainage ditch called – with some irony – the Bussex Rhine. Churchill commanded the Royal foot – five battalions of hardened troops, including both regiments of the Foot Guards. A small force of Royal cavalry guarded the crossing over the ditch to the east. The battle began at around 1.30am on 6 July.

The Duke of Monmouth divided his 4,000 men into five regiments, and supported them with a small detachment of cavalry. Unable to cross the ditch, both sides lined up on opposite sides of it and blazed away with their muskets. It was a firefight the veterans were bound to win, although at one stage Dumbarton's Scottish regiment were hard pressed. Churchill redeployed two of his line battalions to the right wing to support them, while Feversham split his cavalry into two bodies, and sent them to either side, with orders to cross the ditch and then fall on the rebel flanks.

By that stage the rebels were already pulling back – driven off by the firepower of Churchill's infantry. He ordered his grenadiers to advance, using planks to ford the ditch. Using them as a shield, he set about moving the rest of his small army over the obstacle. By that time, however, the battle was over, and the rebels were in full flight. Monmouth was captured two days later, and a week after that he was beheaded in front of the Tower of London. King James' retaliation was brutal – over 300 captured rebels were executed, and hundreds more were deported as slaves. While the Earl of Feversham claimed full credit for Sedgemoor, it was widely acknowledged that it was rightfully Churchill's victory.

The Glorious Revolution

It seems that King James II and VII had learned little from the execution of his father. While his informants told him that Protestant resentment of him was on the increase, he continued to flaunt his faith and appoint Roman Catholics to positions of power. He declared himself above the law. For his part John Churchill remained loyal to his royal master, but he clung to his Protestant beliefs, and kept an increasingly low profile at court. In June 1688 Queen Mary gave birth to a son – James – which raised the possibility of a Catholic succession. Enough was enough. At that point a group of Protestant noblemen invited Prince William of Orange to intervene, and to claim the throne for his own. Not only was the Dutch stadholder a Protestant, but he was also married to Mary Stuart, King James' eldest daughter. Through her he had a viable, if not wholly legitimate, claim to the throne.

Prince William landed at Brixham in Devon in mid-November 1688. Later, British historians dubbed what followed as a 'Glorious Revolution' as a way of whitewashing the fact that this was in essence a foreign invasion, albeit one launched at the behest of a cabal of English Protestants. In truth there was little glorious about the affair, which was more an exercise in brinkmanship than revolution. King James ordered the Earl of Feversham to muster the Royal army at Salisbury, and Churchill was expected to join it. After all, the King had promoted him to the rank of lieutenant-general only a week before, and given him command of his infantry. Churchill, however, had already decided to betray his royal master.

Churchill realized that the Royal army had little stomach for a fight. William was advancing from Devon with an army of 15,000 experienced Dutch soldiers, and the men in the Royal army were as divided in their loyalties as Churchill. Desertion was rife, many officers planned to defect at the first opportunity and few soldiers wanted to fight fellow Protestants on behalf of a Catholic monarch. Set against Churchill's religion was his long association with James. He owed the King everything, and betraying him must have been one of the hardest decisions he ever made. In the end he attended the King's council of war on 23 November, and that evening he rode out of the camp and headed for William's army, which had reached Axminster. He left behind a letter to James, which apologized profusely for his actions, but claimed that he was acting on a higher principle than mere personal loyalty. His true loyalty was to his religion.

King James declared to Feversham: 'I did not expect this terrible blow' – a desertion by the one man who had a chance of defeating Prince William's Dutch army. The King returned to London to discover that Princess Anne had already fled north to Nottingham, accompanied by Lady Sarah Churchill. 'Even my children have forsaken me' he lamented. He had little option but to flee the country. James paused only to throw his Seal of State into the Thames before making his escape by sea, reaching the safety of France just before Christmas. Feversham disbanded what remained of the army, and on 1 January Churchill was on hand to welcome Prince William into London.

John Churchill (1650–1722), Duke of Marlborough, seen here as a young and aspiring commander in the service of King William III. In fact, William didn't completely trust Churchill, and he preferred to rely on Dutch rather than English field commanders. (Stratford Archive)

While Parliament wrangled over finding a way to make William's reign legitimate, John Churchill resumed his role as gentleman of the bedchamber, albeit serving a new master. He was also reconfirmed as a lieutenant-general in William's service, and given the task of rebuilding the English Army. Prince William also wanted to bestow a fresh honour on the man who had done so much to ease the transition of power. So, on 11 April 1689, the day of the coronation, John Churchill was ennobled, becoming the Earl of Marlborough, a title which had recently become extinct. King William III of England and II of Scotland and his wife Queen Mary II of both countries would rule jointly, but the exiled King James would remain a serious threat, and it was unlikely that both he and his host King Louis XIV of France would acquiesce meekly to this seizure of power. For his part John Churchill, Earl of Marlborough, was viewed with suspicion. After all, he had turned his coat once, and he might do so again. The only way he could overcome this cloud of distrust was to prove his loyalty to King William on the battlefield.

King William III and II (r. 1689–1702), as depicted by Jan Wyck. Churchill's last-minute defection to William in 1688 was probably the general's most controversial and widely criticized decision. (Private Dutch collection)

The War of the Grand Alliance

In May 1689 England, Scotland and Holland jointly declared war on France. This would be a war on two fronts. In April King James II was transported to Ireland by a French fleet, where an Irish Jacobite army had formed and was ready to fight for their Catholic king. The Protestant towns of Londonderry and Enniskillen declared their allegiance to William, and waited for his army to come to their rescue. On the mainland of Europe, French troops were keeping the Austrians and their German allies occupied along the Rhine, while in Flanders (now southern Belgium), a French army was preparing to drive northwards into Holland.

The Dutch Army was commanded by the ageing Prince of Waldeck, and while many of his men were Dutch regulars, other allied contingents were gradually arriving to fight alongside him from Prussia, Sweden, several small German states and from Britain. While King William attempted to deal with King James in Ireland, the Earl of Marlborough was sent to Flanders at the head of an 8,000-strong Anglo-Scottish contingent to join Waldeck's army. The Dutch Prince wasn't impressed by the quality of these reinforcements, but he admired their commander.

On 25 August the Allied army fought their first major battle against the French near the small Flemish town of Walcourt. The Allies were slightly more numerous than their French opponents, but the Duc d'Humières had faith in the quality of his French troops, and launched an attack. The attack was held just outside the town, and at 6.00pm Waldeck launched a two-pronged counter-attack. Marlborough commanded the assault on the Allied left, and charged at the head of the cavalry of the Guard, supported by two battalions of infantry. The French withdrew in disarray, but a powerful cavalry rearguard prevented the Allies from taking full advantage of their victory. The Prince of Waldeck later said of Marlborough that 'despite his youth he displayed greater military capacity than do most generals after a long series of wars'. King William was delighted too, and rewarded Marlborough with a lucrative colonelcy.

In July 1690 King William defeated King James at the battle of the Boyne, and while James fled back to France, William consolidated his grip on Ireland. Marlborough arrived in Ireland soon afterwards, just as William moved the bulk of his veteran troops to Flanders, where Waldeck's army had been defeated by the French at Fleurus. William's first priority was to protect Holland from invasion, but before he left he granted Marlborough permission to launch an assault on the Jacobite strongholds of Cork and Kinsale. Cork was taken by assault in early October, and Kinsale fell a few weeks later. On the face of it, King William should have been delighted. He wrote: 'No officer living who has seen so little service as my Lord Marlborough is so fit for great commands.' Unfortunately, William's primary loyalty was to his Dutch generals, rather than an Englishman who still carried a whiff of disloyalty about him.

King Louis XIV of France (r. 1643–1715) was the richest and most powerful monarch in Europe, but near-constant warfare drained his treasury, and Marlborough felt that a decisive military victory could force Louis to sue for peace. (Bavarian Schlösserverwaltung, Munich)

In late 1691 Marlborough was sent to Holland to help plan a renewed campaign against the French. Then, in January, he was summarily dismissed. The reason was probably the row that erupted between Princess Anne and Queen Mary, with Anne being egged on by Lady Sarah Churchill. Then it was suggested that Marlborough maintained a correspondence with the exiled King James. In May 1692 Marlborough was incarcerated in the Tower of London, facing a charge of high treason. He was released five months later, but was exiled from court, and he and Sarah retired to Holywell House, still bemused by their sudden fall from grace.

Meanwhile, the war wasn't going well for William. Ireland had been pacified, but French victories at Steenkerke (1692) and Neerwinden (1694) meant that Flanders was effectively lost to the Dutch, and the threat of a French invasion of Holland remained. In the end, William made peace with France in 1697. While Marlborough's English supporters pleaded for his reinstatement to the army, William remained adamant. In July 1694 he replied to one plea by writing: 'I do not think it for the good of my service, to entrust the command of my troops to him.' Marlborough would remain in the political wilderness until the death of Queen Mary in January 1695.

Queen Mary was childless when she died, which left Princess Anne as heir to the thrones of England and Scotland. Thanks to the friendship between

The monarchs of the Allied 'Grand Alliance' – Queen Anne of Great Britain, the Holy Roman Emperor Charles VI and King John V of Portugal – surrounded by a triumphal arch bearing the coats of arms of their German and Dutch allies. (Stratford Archive)

Anne and Sarah, Marlborough's fortunes revived as Anne was increasingly seen as the heir apparent. By 1698 Marlborough had been readmitted to court, and while the King remained cold, the prospect of a new war with France meant that Marlborough was needed where he could do the most good. In June 1701 Marlborough was appointed General of Infantry, and Ambassador-Extraordinary to the Dutch Republic. He accompanied King William on a mission to Holland in early 1702, to forge a new military alliance. It was on his return that William fell from his horse after it stumbled on a molehill. Infection set in, and the King died on 8 March 1702. Anne was duly crowned Queen of England and Scotland on 23 April. She inherited a joint kingdom on the brink of war with France, which was finally declared on 15 May. Fortunately, in Marlborough she had the perfect commander. Her leading general had everything arranged, and within weeks he would lead her troops into battle as part of a powerful Allied army. This time though, Marlborough himself would be at its head.

THE HOURS OF DESTINY

Opening moves

John Churchill, Earl of Marlborough, was a man of many parts – a discreet diplomat, a love-struck husband, a suave courtier – but above all he was a soldier. In 1702 he had been away from the battlefield for a decade, and while he still knew his job, he needed a war to prove himself again. Fortunately for him, when the war came, Marlborough would be at its epicentre.

The War of the Spanish Succession (1701–14) came about as a result of the death of King Charles II of Spain in November. The two main rivals for the throne were Louis XIV of France and Emperor Leopold I of Austria. Neither ruler wanted the other to gain control of Spain, nor did William or Anne want Spain to become allied to either France or Austria. Louis' grandson, Philip of Anjou, was declared the rightful successor, becoming Philip V. Austria and France prepared for war, and in the summer of 1701 the two countries came to blows in Italy.

That September, King William proposed the formation of a new alliance, this time incorporating the Austrian Holy Roman Empire as well as the 'Maritime Powers' (England, Scotland, Denmark and Holland), plus Prussia and several of the smaller German States. Bavaria and Spain sided with France, while outside the main theatre Portugal and the Duchy of Savoy offered their support to the Allies. The battle lines were drawn, but while fighting would obviously take place in other theatres, it was clear that the war would be decided in the Spanish Netherlands. Once again, Flanders would become a battlefield.

In May the Earl of Marlborough became the head of the Allied army gathering in Holland. England and Scotland had pledged a total of 40,000 troops, matched by 60,000 Dutch soldiers, and 30,000 men from the German states. On the Rhine the Imperialists (the Austrians) had 90,000 troops, while the French – holding the central position – could draw on 300,000 men. These were deceptive totals – many troops of both sides were scattered in garrisons.

The campaign began in the late summer, with Marlborough moving down the river Meuse (Maas), capturing a string of French-held towns. Venlo fell in late September, followed by Roermond. Liège (Luik) capitulated in mid-October. The French commander was the young Louis, Duke de Bourgogne, supervised by Marshal Boufflers. They regarded these towns as outposts, as their main defensive position – the Lines of Brabant – stretched behind them, from the mouth of the Scheldt estuary to Namur. The French avoided battle, and on the one occasion Marlborough had of bringing on a fight the Dutch vetoed the attack. An irritated Marlborough could do little but make plans for the following year.

Marlborough spent the winter concocting his 'Grand Design', the centrepiece of which was an assault on Antwerp. That would breach the French Lines of Brabant, and give the Allies control of the second-largest city in the Spanish Netherlands. In the end the campaign achieved nothing. A Dutch-led diversion to the east of Antwerp ended in disaster, and while Marlborough regained the initiative by capturing the small fortified towns of Bonn, Huy and Limbourg (Limburg), the French continued to avoid an open battle. It was all hugely disappointing. Marlborough even offered to tender his resignation, but Queen Anne refused to contemplate it. To help assuage her commander, she elevated him from an earl to a duke. Unable to resign, all that was left was to find a way of freeing himself of his over-cautious Dutch politicians, and forcing the enemy to fight.

During the War of the Spanish Succession dragoons were often sent to forage for supplies, or to destroy crops that might be used by the enemy. These horsemen are pictured wearing their characteristic stocking caps. (Bavarian Schlösserverwaltung, Munich)

The Spanish Netherlands 1701–12

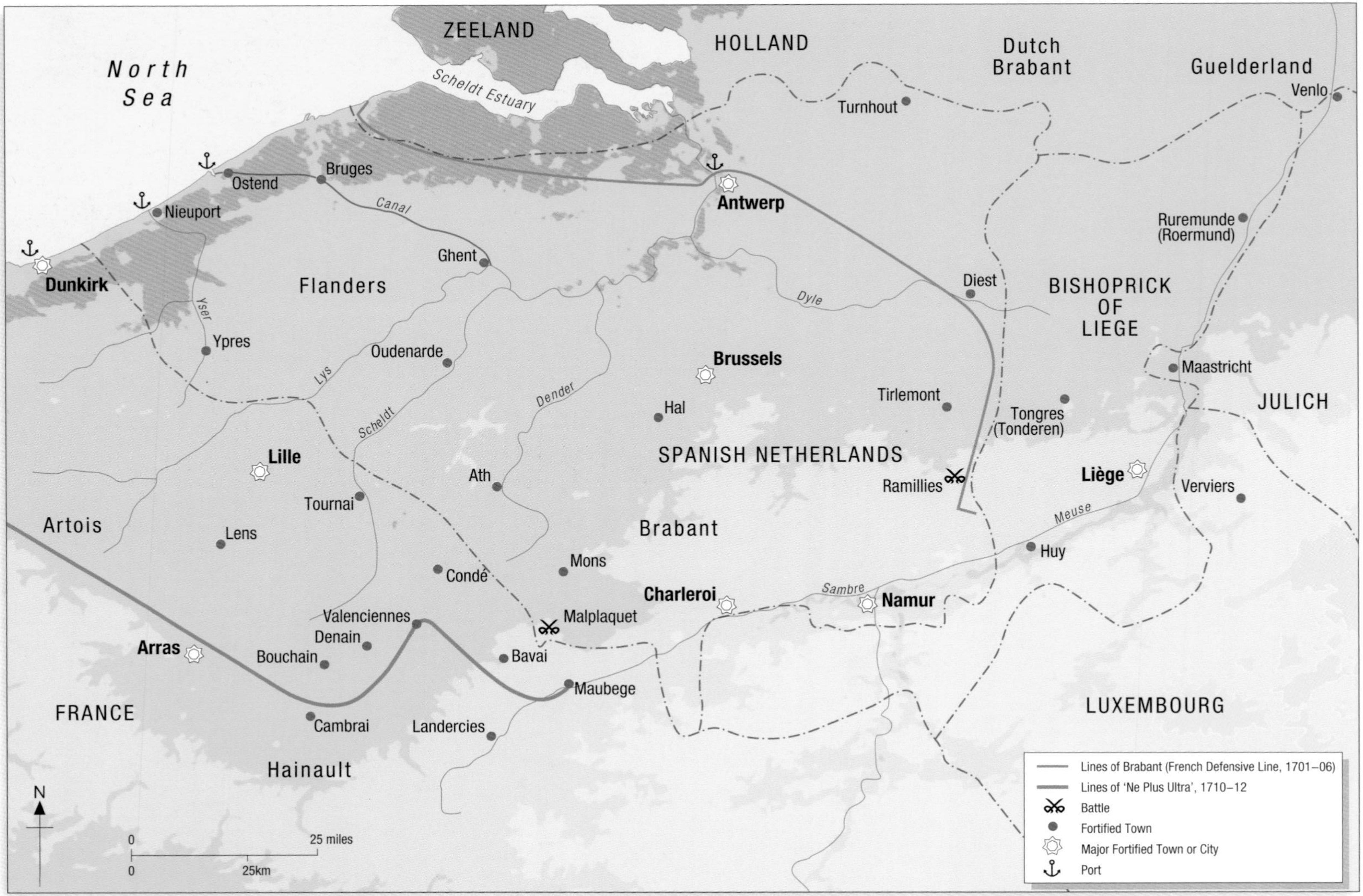

North Sea

ZEELAND

HOLLAND

Guelderland

Dutch Brabant

BISHOPRICK OF LIEGE

JULICH

LUXEMBOURG

SPANISH NETHERLANDS

Brabant

Flanders

Artois

Hainault

FRANCE

Scheldt Estuary

Venlo

Ruremunde (Roermund)

Maastricht

Verviers

Liège

Huy

Tongres (Tonderen)

Diest

Turnhout

Tirlemont

Ramillies

Namur

Antwerp

Brussels

Hal

Charleroi

Mons

Malplaquet

Maubege

Bavai

Landercies

Condé

Ath

Oudenarde

Ghent

Bruges

Ostend

Nieuport

Ypres

Lille

Lens

Tournai

Valenciennes

Denain

Bouchain

Cambrai

Arras

Dunkirk

Dyle

Dendel

Scheldt

Lys

Yser

Canal

Meuse

Sambre

N

0   25 miles
0   25km

Lines of Brabant (French Defensive Line, 1701–06)

Lines of 'Ne Plus Ultra', 1710–12

Battle

Fortified Town

Major Fortified Town or City

Port

Blenheim 1704

The march to the Danube

That winter, it was clear to Marlborough that there was no overall direction to the war, and no coordination between his army and that of the Imperialists, who had been campaigning along the Rhineland and in Northern Italy, accomplishing little. In fact, after Marshal Villars defeated the Imperialists at the battle of Friedlingen (1702) the Austrians had been on the defensive. In 1703 the French managed to link up with the army of Maximilian Emanuel, the elector of Bavaria, and helped the Bavarians clear the Imperialists from Bavarian soil. With their rear secure along the Rhine the French were now considering a strike against Vienna, using Bavaria as a base of operations. There was now a strong possibility that Austria could be forced out of the war.

The situation was so grave that Emperor Leopold recalled Prince Eugene of Savoy from Italy. Eugene had first distinguished himself fighting the Turks, and by 1704 he had become the Empire's most accomplished soldier. The military situation was complex. Two French armies were deployed to the west of the Rhine, with a total strength of more than 50,000 men. Of these, Marshal Tallard's 30,000 men were planning to join forces with the Bavarians for the coming campaign. For his part the elector of Bavaria and Marshal Marsin commanded a Franco-Bavarian force of 45,000 men, deployed in winter garrisons throughout Bavaria. The Imperialist army under Louis, Margrave of Baden, numbered less than 35,000 men, and even the arrival of Eugene of Savoy as his co-commander failed to lift the air of defeat in his camp.

Marlborough finally decided to intervene. By leaving the bulk of the Dutch to defend the Spanish Netherlands, he would march the rest of his army south, down the eastern bank of the Rhine and into Bavaria. There he would join forces with the Imperialists. In an age when armies only moved between supply bases and garrisoned towns, this was an ambitious venture, made all the more so because he had to keep his plan secret in order to prevent it being vetoed by the Dutch. He had already moved his non-Dutch troops to the river Moselle, leaving the Dutch to face the French closer to Antwerp. All he had to do now was to march this 40,000-strong force almost 250 miles (400km).

On 19 May he led his army south from Bedburg, to the west of Cologne, and reached the Rhine near Coblenz a week later. He had only 20,000 troops under his command – soldiers of his own Anglo-Scottish contingent and Allied troops in English pay. At Coblenz he rendezvoused with

Prince François-Eugene of Savoy (1663–1736) was one of the Holy Roman Empire's most gifted field commanders, and certainly its most successful. His military partnership with the Duke of Marlborough produced some of the most spectacular Allied victories of the war. (Stratford Archive)

5,000 Prussian and Hanoverian troops, and two days later he crossed the river to the eastern bank using a pontoon bridge. Marshal Villeroi's spies reported all this to him, but he was perplexed. Why was Marlborough leaving the Spanish Netherlands exposed? Did he plan to attack Bedmar in the Moselle valley? In any case Villeroi had little option but to march south too, but he was unable to match the fast pace of Marlborough's army. Marlborough had a head start, and, unencumbered by a supply train, his men were marching an average of 7½ miles (12km) a day. While this doesn't sound spectacular, Marlborough was able to sustain the march for a long distance, through pre-arranged supply depots. At Frankfurt he even arranged a stockpile of shoes, to replace those worn through on the march. The genius of the operation lay in its detail.

Other German contingents joined him en route, as Marlborough had arranged, and by June the army had swollen to 40,000 men. On 3 June Marlborough's advance guard crossed the river Main near Kastel, and Villeroi was left in no doubt that Marlborough intended to continue into Bavaria. In effect the river Main was Marlborough's Rubicon – once across it he was committed to a campaign along the Danube. South of the Main Marlborough's supply problems eased, as he was advancing closer to the Imperial depots, and he was at last able to open up communications with Baden and Eugene. On 10 June Eugene arrived to liaise between the two armies. The two commanders formed an immediate bond, helped in part by their shared aggressive spirit.

Four days later Marlborough met Louis, Margrave of Baden, at Gross Heppach, a few kilometres east of Stuttgart. Baden was altogether more reserved – a commander who was ruled by caution. While Eugene agreed to watch the Rhine near Baden to prevent the arrival of French reinforcements, Marlborough and Baden agreed to march eastwards towards the elector's army. The elector and Marsin were now encamped 50 miles (80km) to the east at Dillingen, on the banks of the Danube. With a combined force of 60,000 men, Marlborough and Baden outnumbered their opponents by a factor of three to one.

The walls of Donauwörth on the river Danube served as a Franco-Bavarian bastion, preventing Marlborough from crossing the river into Bavaria. By capturing the city and its bridges Marlborough could threaten the enemy's heartland. (Courtesy of Brig. Charles S. Grant)

The Schellenberg

When he learned of Marlborough's approach the elector sent messengers to Versailles demanding French help, but otherwise he remained where he was. Marlborough didn't want to risk a frontal attack on Dillingen. He therefore looked for another crossing into Bavaria. He chose Donauwörth, 25 miles (40km) downstream from Dillingen, which was held by a small Franco-Bavarian force. Its capture would place him in the elector's rear. All he had to do was to capture the town and the fortified hill known as the Schellenberg ('Bell Hill'), which loomed over its eastern side. The Schellenberg was the key to Donauwörth, while the bridge beyond it was Marlborough's key to Bavaria.

Capturing Donauwörth would be no easy matter. The Schellenberg was defended by a Franco-Bavarian Corps of 10,000 men, under the command of the Count d'Arco, the foremost general in the Bavarian army. The elector was well aware of how important Donauwörth was, and he put some of his best troops there. The Allied army reached Donauwörth during the afternoon of 2 July. The men must have gazed up at the Schellenberg with a sense of dread. Marlborough cajoled Baden into agreeing to an immediate assault, and the troops were deployed accordingly, with assault columns of grenadiers formed at the base of the hill and the lines of infantry arrayed behind. The assault force consisted of 6,000 men – the rest of the Allied army remained in reserve.

The advance began shortly before 6.00pm. Allied guns opened up a spirited bombardment, hindered by the extreme elevation of the hilltop. Enemy roundshot crashed through the ranks of the Allies as they clambered up the slope, but the assault columns pressed on. When the Allies reached the summit the French opened fire on them with volleys of musketry, fired at point-blank range. At that moment it looked as if the assault might fail. Scores of men fell in front of the defences, and the attackers wavered. Then, it was discovered that the western slopes of the hill between the town and the summit were defended by just two French battalions, arrayed behind a breastwork of gabions. Marlborough ordered Baden to send in his Imperial infantry, who stormed the defences and surged over the gabions. This was the key moment of the battle.

The defenders on the Schellenberg were now cut off from the town. This also meant that their main line of retreat was cut, leaving just a flimsy pontoon bridge that spanned the river at the base of the hill. The defenders of the hill began to drift away towards safety, and at last the battered assault columns were able to fight their way over the earthworks. At that point the defences crumbled – French and Bavarian infantry began running down the rear slopes of the hill heading for the pontoon bridge. Marlborough halted his infantry on the summit, but he sent his dragoons to pursue the broken enemy. By 8.30pm it was all over, and only Donauwörth itself lay in Bavarian hands. Its defenders tried to set fire to their depots before the Allies could capture it, but the townspeople doused the flames, and the following morning they opened the town gates to Marlborough's army.

Marlborough had captured Donauwörth and its bridge, but the cost had been high. The slopes of the Schellenberg were carpeted with the dead and dying – the Allied casualties alone came to over 5,000 men, dead and wounded. The French and Bavarians suffered too – some 2,000 of them had been taken prisoner, and another 3,000 lay on the summit of the hill or on the slope leading down to the river. Some of those who fled never returned to their units, and less than 3,000 men remained under d'Arco's command when he rejoined the elector's army. Marlborough had won a spectacular but costly victory, where he willingly sacrificed lives in exchange for immediate results.

The battle of Blenheim

The capture of Donauwörth was less fruitful that it could have been because the elector was unlikely to sue for peace. He knew that reinforcements were on their way – Marshal Tallard had bypassed Eugene of Savoy's Imperialists, and was marching from the Rhine to the Danube. Consequently, the elector and Marshal Marsin withdrew to the safety of Augsburg and waited for Tallard's arrival. Marlborough lacked the siege guns he needed to tackle such a well-defended city, so instead he sent his troops into the Bavarian countryside, ravaging it by burning crops and villages, a move designed to reduce Bavaria's enthusiasm for the conflict. Marlborough was criticized for such unchivalrous tactics, but he was fighting to win, not to conform to some gentlemanly code of military conduct. These depredations had the added effect of splitting the Franco-Bavarian army, as the elector detached as many as 15,000 troops to protect his own estates and other key locations across Bavaria.

Marshal Tallard had 34,000 troops under his command, but his march through the Black Forest was fraught with difficulty. Disease ('German Sickness') amongst his horses meant that thousands of them died by the roadside, reducing his cavalry strength by as much as a third. Enraged by French pillaging, the local peasantry took their revenge by butchering stragglers and foraging parties. One officer in Tallard's army reported that: 'The enraged peasantry eventually killed several thousand of our men before the army was clear of the Black Forest.' Despite all these difficulties Tallard made good progress, crossing the Danube at Ulm, and rendezvoused with the elector and Marsin near Augsburg on 6 August.

Eugene of Savoy had been outmanoeuvred when Marshal Villeroi feinted against the Imperial defences on the Rhine, allowing Tallard to cross the river without hindrance. He left 15,000 men on the Rhine and marched 13,000 men eastwards, shadowing Tallard. On reaching the Danube, Eugene continued

In this stylized depiction of the battle of Blenheim, the engagement is seen from the Austrian perspective, with Eugene rather than Marlborough portrayed as the arbiter of victory. In fact both Allied commanders willingly shared the laurels. (Galleria Sabauda, Turin)

along its northern bank to Höchstädt. He then rode ahead to confer with Marlborough and Baden. The three commanders concluded that the situation was still very favourable. The Franco-Bavarians, now under the overall command of Tallard, had approximately 56,000 men at their disposal. Including Eugene's contingent, the Allies had around 71,000.

On the face of it, Marlborough's next decision made no military sense. It was decided that Louis would take 15,000 men and capture Ingolstadt, 30 miles (48km) east of Donauwörth. While the town on the Danube was an important Bavarian supply depot, it flew in the face of military logic to divide the army if battle was imminent. However, Marlborough and Eugene wanted rid of their cautious co-commander, and felt the loss of 15,000 men a justifiable sacrifice in the circumstances. Baden never forgave them their duplicity.

On 11 August Eugene's small force united with the advance guard of Marlborough's army near Donauwörth. This gave the Allies a combined strength of 56,000 men – a similar total to the French. On 12 August the two commanders climbed the church tower in the small village of Tapfheim and saw the French army encamped about 3 miles (5km) away, on the far side of the Nebel stream, halfway between Tapfheim and Höchstädt, on the north bank of the Danube. As soon as they clambered down to ground level they began preparing for a battle the following morning.

The Franco-Bavarian army was deployed behind the Nebel stream, with its left flank close to the village of Lützingen, where the river valley rose up into wooded hills, and its right anchored on the village of Blenheim, within musket shot of the river Danube. The villages of Oberglau and Unterglau lay between Lützingen and Blenheim, each village approximately a mile (1.6km) away from the other, thereby forming a string of fortifiable villages along the line of the Nebel. It also meant that Tallard's army had to hold a front 4 miles (6.5km) long. This mightn't have been the best place for the army to deploy for battle – more suitable terrain could be found closer to Tapfheim or Höchstädt. However, Tallard, Marsin and the elector never thought that Marlborough would attack them.

The site was chosen more because it provided the army with a dry encampment close to a stream than because the terrain was well suited to defence. That said, according to military dictum, Tallard deployed his army in line of battle, with the troops of the elector and Marshal Marsin on his left, his own infantry on the right, and the bulk of the French cavalry in the centre, between Oberglau and Blenheim. Unterglau was ignored as it lay on the far side of the Nebel stream, but the remaining villages were fortified, where they could act as bastions.

The Allied army deployed in front of Tapfheim well before dawn on 13 August, then advanced in battle formation towards the French line. It took the best part of six hours to advance the intervening 2 miles (3km), but as the early morning mist cleared the French finally saw the Allies approaching them from the east. The Allies' approach came as a total surprise – tents were trampled and breakfasts scattered as the Franco-Bavarian army scrambled to form themselves into line of battle.

The Nebel stream near Unterglau was hardly a major obstacle, but it did force any attacker to halt and reorder their ranks after crossing it. Unterglau is just off the picture to the left. (Courtesy of Brig. Charles S. Grant)

The Allies arrayed themselves on the far side of the Nebel, about a kilometre from the waiting Franco-Bavarian line. Prince Eugene commanded the right wing facing Lutzheim and Oberglau, while on his left Marlborough's younger brother Charles Churchill commanded the centre, supported by most of Marlborough's cavalry. Marlborough grouped the bulk of the British and Hanovarian contingents on the far left. Marlborough hoped to drain the centre of French troops, and then launch a decisive strike against the French centre with the bulk of his cavalry.

The battle began a little before 12.30pm as Lord Cutts on the left wing launched an attack on Blenheim. The British reached the palisades before being driven back by heavy fire. The British and Hanovarians pulled back, re-formed and then attacked again, but once more they were unable to breach the defences. By this time the village had been reinforced by troops drawn from the French centre. This was exactly what Marlborough had hoped would happen.

To support the second attack Lord Cutts ordered his British cavalry into action. They were counter-charged by the Gendarmes de France, one of the most prestigious French regiments. Brigadier Palmes' outnumbered horse routed their French opponents, and then withdrew in the face of French infantry fire and cavalry manoeuvring. Marlborough ordered Cutts to hold his men back rather than launch a third attack. The battle for Blenheim

Conference between Marlborough and Eugene before Blenheim

One of the great military partnerships in history began on 10 June 1704, when the Duke of Marlborough and Prince Eugene of Savoy met for the first time in Mundelsheim, a small village near Stuttgart. Just over two months later the two commanders spent the early morning of 13 August planning their attack against the Franco-Bavarian army encamped near Blenheim. Shortly before 7.00am they rode past the village of Wolperstetten to peer through the morning mist at the enemy, who occupied the high ground on the far side of the Nebel stream. They were accompanied by Major-General Natzmer, the commander of the Prussian cavalry, whose experienced eyes confirmed that the slope in front of them was suitable for cavalry, if only the Allied horse were able to cross the stream. This view of the scene shows Marlborough in the centre, with Prince Eugene on his left listening to Natzmer's appreciation of the terrain, which was delivered in broken French. Behind Marlborough stands one of his messengers, wearing a distinctive jockey cap and blue-and-white livery. Shortly after 7.00am Prince Eugene and Natzmer rode off towards the west, leaving Marlborough to supervise the final deployment of the Allied left wing.

Blenheim village, viewed from the Höchstädt–Donauwörth road, which crossed the battlefield a little to the west of the village. Lord Cutts' infantry assaulted the heavily defended village from the left of this viewpoint. (Courtesy of Brig. Charles S. Grant)

village developed into an exchange of musketry, but now the bulk of the French foot were pinned in the village, unable to intervene anywhere else. Prince Eugene was having a tough time in front of Oberglau and Lutzingen. The first assault on Oberglau was driven back, and while Eugene's horse and foot launched repeated supporting attacks over the Nebel, all of these assaults were repulsed. By mid-afternoon Eugene had made no headway. Again though, these Allied attacks helped to pin the enemy in place, and even to drain troops from the centre.

At 3.00pm Marlborough felt that the time was right to launch his main attack in the centre. Throughout the battle his infantry there had been lying down in order to reduce the effectiveness of enemy artillery. Pioneers laid fascines in the stream, creating crossing points for the Allied horse, while the Allied guns pounded the French centre. An hour before, Marshal Tallard had ridden over to the left flank to confer with Marshal Marsin. He was therefore unaware that the Marquis de Clérambault commanding the defenders of Blenheim had moved the French reserve from the centre to the right flank.

This impressive diorama of the battle of Blenheim is currently on display in the Schloss Höchstädt, and shows the climax of the battle in the late afternoon. In this view Orkney's infantry are seen encircling Blenheim village. (Courtesy of Brig. Charles S. Grant)

Blenheim was the perfect example of Marlborough's battle-winning tactic, which he would repeat with some success at Ramillies (1706) and Malplaquet (1709). By threatening the enemy flanks he encouraged the enemy to weaken their centre, allowing him to launch a smashing blow against the middle of the enemy line. When he gave the signal, a mass of troops surged forward over the stream – 19 battalions of foot and 81 squadrons of horse. All the French had left to oppose them between Oberglau and Blenheim were nine battalions of raw infantry and 64 bloodied squadrons of cavalry.

The French cavalry counter-charged to buy time, but the French horse were soon forced to retire. Now it was the turn of the Allied cavalry to suffer at the hands of infantry – the remaining nine battalions that comprised the French reserve. Tallard rode up and ordered his cavalry to counter-charge again. They refused. That was his last chance of snatching victory from defeat. Veteran British and Hanovarian infantry soon dispersed the French infantry, and at 5.30pm the Allied horse swept forward again. The remaining French horse broke and ran, and Tallard was taken prisoner. The Earl of Orkney then ordered his infantry to link up with Cutts' men, and to surround Blenheim village.

On the French left wing the defenders were powerless to intervene. Marshal Marsin and the elector ordered their infantry to abandon the two villages and to pull back in good order, hoping to save what they could from the debacle. Prince Eugene's men surged forward and then re-formed beyond the burning villages. His exhausted men then halted, unable to do more.

While the Allied cavalry pursued the remains of the French horse, Marlborough turned his attention to Blenheim. Many of the French troops were so crowded together that they couldn't even lift their muskets. Lord Orkney and Lord Cutts ordered their men to fire into the crowded village, while Allied dragoons moved around the back of it to seal off the last avenue of escape. Many Frenchmen tried to swim across the Danube, but most remained where they were, a disordered mob. A breakout might have been possible if Clérambault had acted swiftly, but he had disappeared – possibly drowning in an attempt to swim to safety. When their powder ran out the French opened negotiations with the Allies, and at 9.00pm the remnants of the French infantry surrendered. Marlborough's victory was complete.

Blenheim Church marks the centre of the old village, and was the scene of the final French surrender. Many French regiments burned their standards first, rather than let them fall into enemy hands. (Courtesy of Brig. Charles S. Grant)

Over 20,000 French and Bavarian troops lay on the battlefield that night – dead and wounded – intermingled with 13,000 Allies. While the cost in lives was high, Marlborough had won a spectacular victory. Some 14,000 prisoners had been taken, 60 guns had been captured and the remnants of the French army were in headlong flight. While the fighting around Blenheim was still raging, Marlborough grabbed a scrap of paper – a tavern receipt – and penned a note to Duchess Sarah. It read: 'I have no time to say more, but beg you will give my duty to the Queen, and let her know her army has had a glorious victory. Marshal Tallard and two other generals are in my coach, and I am following the rest.' Even in the moment of victory, he found time to think of his wife.

This was the most complete of victories, and Marlborough and Eugene deserved the laurels. The French had not been defeated in a major battle for four decades. Blenheim shattered their aura of invincibility. Vienna was saved and Bavaria was knocked out of the war. With hindsight we can see that it marked a turning point in French fortunes. After Blenheim the French were on the defensive, and although the war would drag on for another decade, the French would never recover the initiative. Queen Anne was delighted. She granted

The battle of Blenheim, 13 August 1704

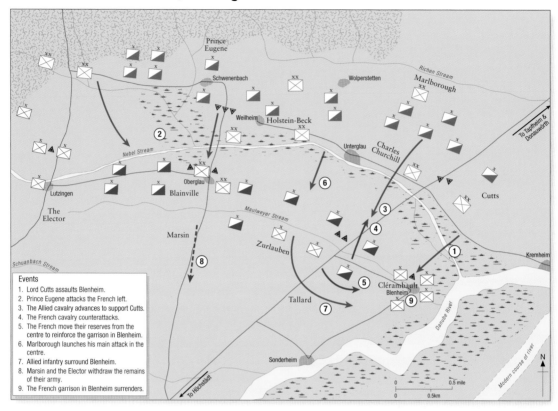

Events
1. Lord Cutts assaults Blenheim.
2. Prince Eugene attacks the French left.
3. The Allied cavalry advances to support Cutts.
4. The French cavalry counterattacks.
5. The French move their reserves from the centre to reinforce the garrison in Blenheim.
6. Marlborough launches his main attack in the centre.
7. Allied infantry surround Blenheim.
8. Marsin and the Elector withdraw the remains of their army.
9. The French garrison in Blenheim surrenders.

Marlborough the royal manor and surrounding estate at Woodstock outside Oxford as a sign of gratitude, and announced that her victorious commander would build a palace there, paid for from the royal treasury. The Queen also granted Marlborough the princely allowance of £5,000 a year for the rest of his life. Above all, Marlborough's military reputation was assured. From that moment on he was seen as the foremost soldier in Europe.

The battle of Blenheim, by the Dutch artist Jan van Huchtenburgh. Rather inaccurately, it follows contemporary artistic convention by having Marlborough observe events unfold from a convenient hill, rather than from the meadow above the Nebel. (Bavarian Army Museum, Ingoldstadt)

Ramillies 1706

Stalemate in Flanders

After his victory, Marlborough marched his original force north to the river Moselle (Mosel), where his army went into winter quarters. He then went on a tour of the German states, taking advantage of the victory to guarantee their continued support. He also laid plans for the campaign of 1705, when he hoped to advance down the Moselle to Metz, and from there to breach France's frontier defences. News also reached him from England. While the country was jubilantly celebrating the victory, there were dissenters, who favoured peace rather than a costly war. The Lord High Treasurer was Marlborough's friend Sidney Godolphin, who, like Marlborough, was a Tory. Nevertheless he advised Marlborough to court the Whig opposition, who were beginning to make political headway. He also told Marlborough that Duchess Sarah and Queen Anne were no longer on such intimate terms as before, and urged Marlborough to encourage his wife to show more caution.

French propagandists had labelled Blenheim an aberration – a rare upset in the natural order of things. In 1705 it might have seemed like they had a point. The Dutch remained cautious, and as the campaigning season opened it was clear that Marshal Villars was ready to block any move down the Moselle. The Imperialists failed to provide Marlborough with the troops he needed, so it was probably with relief that he returned to Flanders, where Marshal Villeroi had captured Huy and was threatening Liège. Marlborough didn't know it then, but all his remaining campaigns would be fought in the region.

Huy was recaptured in July, and Marlborough turned his attention to the Lines of Brabant. By breaching its defences he would undermine the French position in Flanders, and he might even bring the French to battle. In July Marlborough forced a passage through the Lines of Brabant at Elixheim

Prince Eugene leading a charge during the battle of Blenheim, in a detail from a spirited but largely inaccurate painting of the battle by the German artist August Querfurt. It features the Imperialist commander's assault on Oberglau. (Staatliche Schlösser Baden-Württemberg)

An army encampment, in a scene from *Les Excercises de Mars*, a Franco-German military manual dated from 1700. In the foreground a soldier is forced to 'run the gauntlet' of his stick-wielding comrades as a punishment, watched by officers and infantrymen. (Stratford Archive)

(Eliksem) near Louvain (Leuven). Unfortunately Marlborough's Dutch representatives refused to sanction any further advance. The campaign ended in stalemate, largely because the Dutch allowed their over-cautious politicians to dictate the course of military operations.

That winter Marlborough bitterly considered his options. He even contemplated moving his army to Italy, but the move was rejected by everyone but the Imperialists. The French had weathered the disaster of Blenheim, and while Louis XIV was considering making overtures of peace, his military advisors talked him into continuing the fight. During the winter the French rebuilt their armies, and by the spring they were ready to launch an offensive in Flanders, hoping to erase the shame of Blenheim.

Approach to battle

The campaigning season began well for the French. Marshal Villars managed to drive Louis of Baden out of Alsace and back across the Rhine. In Italy, Marshal Vendôme defeated a smaller Imperial army at Calcinato. In Flanders, Marshal Villeroi was encamped near Leuven with 60,000 men, and for once the French were eager for battle. Marsin was poised to march north from Metz with another army if Villeroi managed to defeat Marlborough. Marlborough's 62,300 men were based at Tongres (Tongeren), midway between Maastricht and Leuven. Then, on 15 May, word reached him that Villeroi was on the march.

The scene was set for another decisive clash. Marlborough was aware that Marsin was moving north, and he wanted to attack Villeroi before the two French armies could unite. He marched towards Elixheim, where the lines had been broken the previous year and had never been rebuilt. When he learned of this Villeroi marched south too. Both sides were unclear exactly where the enemy was. On 22 May Villeroi approached the village of Ramillies, a few miles south of Tirlemont (Tienen). Marlborough was less than a day's march to the east, at the hamlet of Corswarem, a few miles to the east. Marlborough reached the ruined Lines of Brabant that afternoon, while

Villeroi ordered his army to make camp on the west bank of the stream called the Little Geete, near the village of Ramillies. Marlborough let his army rest, but he sent Lord Cadogan forward to reconnoitre.

Early on the morning of 23 May Cadogan encountered a French patrol outside Merdorp, and realized that the enemy army must be close by. A thick mist hid the French from view, but by the time Marlborough reached Merdorp the mist had begun to clear and Villeroi's army was revealed, standing to arms on the far bank of the Little Geete. While his army was hurried forward, Marlborough inspected the enemy lines, and decided on his plan of attack. Attack he must, as the French were in a strong defensive position, and therefore unlikely to make the first move.

The battle of Ramillies

The French position ran in a large concave curve, stretching the 3 miles (5km) from the village of Autre Église in the north to Taviers and the river Mehaigne in the south. The village of Ramillies lay in the middle, and north of it ran the Little Geete, a boggy stream lined with trees. Ramillies, Autre Église and the village of Offus, which lay between them, all sat back from the stream on the higher ground to the west. To the south of Ramillies stretched a flat plain, pierced only by the occasional village, and by the prehistoric mound known as the Tomb of Ottomond.

Marshal Villeroi deployed his troops in a conventional manner, with the Bavarian troops of the exiled elector on his extreme right, cavalry interspersed with infantry between Taviers and Ramillies and a solid infantry line on the higher ground to the north, with a reserve of cavalry and infantry behind. On a map it might have looked like a strong defence, but the French were badly spread out, which made it hard to move reserves from one flank to the other.

Marlborough's army deployed on the high ground to the east was more compact, allowing him to concentrate his attacks. In addition, he enjoyed a preponderance of artillery. He also had another advantage – terrain. Just before where the flat land to the east sloped down towards the Little Geete there was a long fold in the ground – a shallow re-entrant. In effect it was a false ridgeline, with a dip behind it. Marlborough recognized that this gave him the opportunity to move troops between his left and his centre without the French observing him. He would make full use of this advantage in the hours that followed.

At 11.00am the Allied artillery opened up a cannonade on Ramillies that lasted for three hours. Thirty 24-pdr guns were ranged against the village, which by early afternoon was little more than a heap of blood-soaked rubble. Then, around 2.00pm, Marlborough launched attacks against the extremities of the French line. In the south the Dutch Guards cleared the French and Bavarians from the village of Franquenée, and then followed up the attack with an assault on Taviers. French dragoons tried to dismount and use firepower to halt the attackers, but the supporting Allied cavalry simply rode them down.

In the north the Earl of Orkney led 12 English and Scottish battalions across the Little Geete. Marshal Villeroi had his headquarters near Offus, and after

The view from the edge of Autre Église village, looking south towards Offus over the ground occupied by the Earl of Orkney's troops. The Little Geete is off to the left of this viewpoint. (Courtesy of Brig. Charles S. Grant)

Blenheim he had been warned that the presence of English troops indicated the location of Marlborough's main attack. Consequently he ordered troops from his centre to reinforce his left flank. While some historians have suggested that Orkney's attack was a feint, contemporary letters and accounts suggest that Marlborough considered it more of a strong probe hoping to break the French line, or at least to pin it in place. The marshy ground along the Little Geete prevented Orkney from supporting his attack with cavalry, but against the odds he managed to fight his way into Autre Église, where his men defied all French attempts to dislodge them.

Another advance in the centre was less successful, as General Schulenburg assaulted Ramillies but was unable to drive the defenders from the ruined village. General Overkirk moved his Allied cavalry up in support, sweeping forward across the open ground. The French guard cavalry, the Maison du Roi, launched a spirited counter-charge which smashed through the first two lines of Allied cavalry, only to be halted by a brigade of Schulenburg's command. It was the critical moment – unless reinforcements arrived the French could win the cavalry mêlée, ride over Schulenburg's infantry, and so win the day. This, of course, was when Marlborough displayed a touch of genius.

Some 38 squadrons of cavalry were arrayed on the hill overlooking the Little Geete, on the Allied right flank. Unable to support Orkney, they simply stood there, waiting for orders. When they came, Marlborough asked them to retire slowly over the brow of the hill into the re-entrant. He then moved them to Ramillies, where they moved forward to support the beleaguered Allied horse. Their arrival gave Marlborough a crucial five-to-three advantage in numbers of cavalry. Just as importantly, these cavalry reinforcements were fresh, and eager for the fray.

The timing was critical. Count Ouwerkerk's four successive lines of cavalry were in trouble. Two of them had been smashed through by the Maison du Roi, while the remainder had been pushed back. To buy time for his reinforcements to arrive, Marlborough rode over to the cavalry mêlée with his staff, hoping that his presence would help steady the Allied troopers. He took part in two charges – the job of a brigadier rather than a commanding general – and in the second he was thrown from his horse and almost trampled on in the swirl of horses, men and dust. Fortunately his staff rushed to his aid, while a regiment of Swiss infantry in Dutch service advanced to cover him. An aide gave Marlborough a spare horse, but as he was mounting it a roundshot whistled between the general's legs, killing the major who was holding his horse steady. It was the closest Marlborough came to death on the battlefield.

By that time the reinforcements had arrived, and it was the turn of the French cavalry to be pushed back. The Maison du Roi were caught in the front and flank by a brigade of Danish cavalry and driven from the field. At that point the embattled French gave way, and pulled back to a new line, stretching between Ramillies and the Tomb of Ottomond. Some 9,000 French and

The battle of Ramillies, 23 May 1706

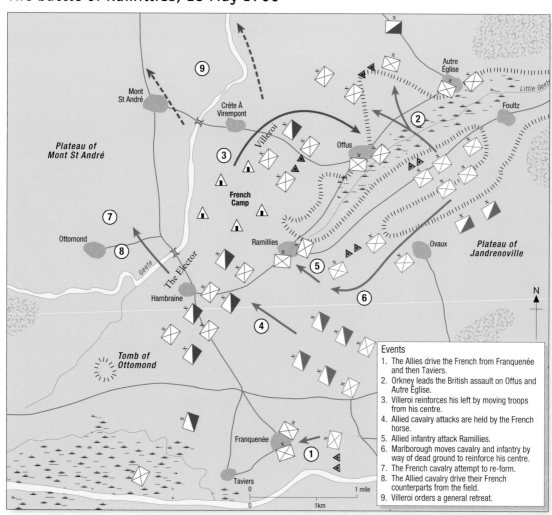

Events
1. The Allies drive the French from Franquenée and then Taviers.
2. Orkney leads the British assault on Offus and Autre Église.
3. Villeroi reinforces his left by moving troops from his centre.
4. Allied cavalry attacks are held by the French horse.
5. Allied infantry attack Ramillies.
6. Marlborough moves cavalry and infantry by way of dead ground to reinforce his centre.
7. The French cavalry attempt to re-form.
8. The Allied cavalry drive their French counterparts from the field.
9. Villeroi orders a general retreat.

While this contemporary engraving of the battle of Ramillies might not be an accurate representation, it does capture some of the flavour of the hard-fought cavalry clash, which took place in the fields to the south and west of Ramillies. (Stratford Archive)

15,000 Allied cavalry had taken part in the great mêlée, and both sides were winded. The fighting subsided a little around 5.00pm, as the fury of the cavalrymen exhausted itself.

At 3.30pm the Earl of Orkney had been ordered to abandon his hard-won bridgehead over the Little Geete, abandoning Autre Église to the French. It was a tough decision, and one that obviously rankled with Orkney. However, it was clear that this was not going to be where the battle was won – Marlborough had already seen how the French centre had been stripped of troops, so he decided that he would launch his killer blow there. When Orkney's men reluctantly recrossed the Little Geete, Marlborough ordered half of them to continue up the hill and into the re-entrant. Then, the battalions were ordered to leave their colour parties where they were while the rest of the men re-emerged in front of Ramillies. By leaving the flags still waving, Marlborough was able to give the impression that the units were still on the hill opposite Offus and Autre Église, thereby making the French unwilling to strip troops from their own left flank.

With these reinforcements Schulenburg launched another assault, and shortly after 6.00pm he managed to drive the Irish 'Wild Geese' out of Ramillies. The French were back as far as Offus, and Villeroi tried to establish a new line anchored on Autre Église. Meanwhile the Allied cavalry charged again, and within minutes the French cavalry broke and ran. They were hindered by the tents and baggage of the French camp, and soon the infantry joined the flight, with whole brigades fleeing the field. Marlborough's cavalry and dragoons gave chase, and the pursuit continued as far as Meldert, some 12 miles (20km) away to the north. As darkness fell Marlborough called off the pursuit, by which time he had already scribbled another note telling both the Queen and Duchess Sarah of his great victory.

This time the cost of Marlborough's victory had been fairly light. At Ramillies the Allies lost just over 1,000 men killed and another 2,500 wounded – a quarter of the casualties lost at Blenheim. He inflicted over 13,000 casualties on the French – dead, wounded or captured – a total that also included losses to their Bavarian and Spanish allies, whose small contingents fought alongside them. Marshal Villeroi and the elector of Bavaria both narrowly escaped being captured during the retreat, but that was little consolation to the commanders who would have to account for their failure to Louis XIV.

The most significant result of Ramillies was that the French defence lines in the Spanish Netherlands had been breached, and what was left of the French field army was streaming towards the French border. The cities of the Spanish Netherlands lay virtually undefended. As Marlborough himself put it: 'We have now the whole summer before us, and with the blessing of God, I shall make the best use of it.' In a letter to Sarah he added: 'I hope I shall do more in this campaign than was done in the last ten years' war in this country.'

During the next few weeks Marlborough sent his men westwards through Flanders, and the poorly defended towns fell one after the other. Louvain fell on 25 May and Brussels the day after, less than two weeks after the victory at Ramillies. Other cities followed in quick succession – Malines, Ghent, Damme, Oudenarde, Bruges and Brussels. The port of Ostend fell on 4 July, providing Marlborough with a vital supply base. Only Dendermonde held out, until Marlborough could bring up his siege train, at which point the garrison capitulated. By that time though, the Allies had captured most of the Spanish Netherlands, leaving the French scrambling desperately to form a new line.

The battle of Ramillies, with Marlborough and his staff in the foreground. French cavalry and Allied infantry mêlée behind them, while in the background the main Allied assault on Ramillies is under way. This was the critical moment of the battle. (Stratford Archive)

The resistance of Dendermonde highlighted the strengthening of French resolve. After his defeat Marshal Villeroi retreated to Cortrai, where he reorganized his shattered army. Reinforcements helped – Marsin arrived from the Moselle with about 16,000 men, while Louis XIV ordered other fronts to be stripped of troops in order to reinforce his army in Flanders. Marshal Vendôme was recalled from Italy to replace the disgraced Villeroi, and garrisons were sent to the cities that still held out in the Spanish Netherlands. By August the French had established a new defensive line which

The Duke of Marlborough and his staff at Ramillies, in a detail from an 18th-century depiction of the battle. Marlborough is pictured in red, while the staff officer in blue is Major-General Armstrong, his gifted Chief of Engineers. (Stratford Archive)

stretched from Ypres (Wervik) to Lille, Tournai and Mons to reach the river Sambre. From there it followed the south bank of the river as it flowed westwards to Namur, the eastern anchor of the French line.

At that point the Allies disagreed about what to do next. Marlborough tried to persuade the Dutch to maintain the initiative, hoping to bypass the French line by marching down the coast. Apart from the capture of Ostend, this scheme came to nothing. On 18 August Marlborough captured Menin, and after the fall of Dendermonde on 5 September, the last major siege of the year was Ath, which he captured on 2 October. Thus ended a spectacular campaign. However, while all this was a great boost for the Allies, the French remained in the war, and the fighting would continue.

Marlborough at Ramillies

During the battle of Ramillies, the Allies spent the early afternoon launching infantry attacks against the French flanks, while in the plain to the south of Ramillies the main cavalry forces of both armies remained stationary. It was after 3.30pm when Marlborough finally unleashed his cavalry, and soon the ground to the south of the village was a swirling mass of horsemen. The French soon rallied from the Allied assault, and their counter-attack – spearheaded by the elite Maison du Roi – drove the Danish and Dutch horsemen back in confusion. Marlborough ordered his cavalry reserves forward, and to win time for them to arrive he rode forward, hoping to rally his flagging troopers. Instead he was knocked from his horse, and for a few minutes he was in grave danger of being killed or captured. A quick-thinking Dutch commander ordered a regiment of Swiss infantry to advance to protect the Allied commander, while Captain Molesworth of Marlborough's staff helped his shaken commander to his feet and led him to safety behind the Swiss line. A fresh horse was found, and minutes later Marlborough was back in the saddle, directing the cavalry reinforcements whose arrival turned the tide of battle.

Oudenarde 1708

A year of frustration

These trees mark the location of the Tomb of Ottomond, the burial mound that marked the site of the second cavalry clash at Ramillies, where the Allied horse broke the hastily assembled French reserves. (Courtesy of Brig. Charles S. Grant)

Marlborough's year of victory was followed by a year of disappointment. Louis XIV tried to open peace negotiations, but the triumphant Allies were having none of it, unless the French abandoned all dynastic claims to Spain. During 1706 the Imperialists had won a victory at Turin, which effectively cleared the French from much of Northern Italy. Plans were laid to build on this success in 1707 by staging an invasion of Provence, supported by an Anglo-Dutch fleet. Prince Eugene was sent to Italy to lead the offensive, and consequently Marlborough was starved of the German troops he needed to campaign effectively in Flanders. In the end Eugene advanced as far as Toulon, where a combination of disease and French reinforcements caused him to lift the siege and withdraw to Italy.

On the Rhine, Marshal Villars launched his own offensive, driving Louis of Baden from the 'impregnable' Lines of Stollhoffen and raiding deep into Germany. In Spain, an Anglo-Portuguese army commanded by the Earl of Galway was soundly defeated by a Franco-Spanish army commanded by the Duke of Berwick. James, Duke of Berwick, was an illegitimate son of James II and VII, produced by James' liaison with Marlborough's sister, Arabella Churchill, when she was the Duke of York's mistress over three decades earlier. Consequently British reinforcements were diverted from Flanders to Spain.

The term British – not English or Scottish – is important. On 1 May 1707 the Act of Union was passed. England and Scotland were no more and the United Kingdom of Great Britain was created in their place. However momentous this might have been politically, it made very little practical difference to Marlborough. After all, Scottish and English regiments had been fighting alongside each other for years – all that happened was that their flags changed, with the Scottish saltire and English St George's cross replaced by the new Union flag. In Flanders the French remained on the defensive, and, short of troops, Marlborough was outnumbered by Marshal Vendôme's French. The summer passed fruitlessly, and Marlborough could do little but make plans for the following year.

While the winter might have been uneventful in Flanders, across the French border at Dunkirk a fleet was gathering, and 12 battalions of French troops were crowded onto transport ships. Louis XIV had decided to back a Jacobite attempt to invade Britain. James II and VII had died in 1701, but his son James, born in 1688, planned to recover his father's kingdoms by force. To the British loyal to Queen Anne he was 'The Pretender'. The invasion fleet sailed in March 1708, bound for the Firth of Forth near Edinburgh. They were shadowed by a Royal Naval fleet commanded by Admiral Byng, who prevented any landing. By the end of April the French were back in Dunkirk, having achieved nothing.

If they had landed – if the Royal Navy had been less vigilant – Marlborough would have had to send troops to Scotland to deal with the Jacobites, and his next battlefield triumph might never have happened.

Marlborough outwitted

In 1708, the 110,000 men who comprised the Franco-Spanish field army in Flanders had two commanders. Louis, Duc de Bourgogne, had almost no military experience, but he was Louis XIV's grandson, and was duly given command of the army. To help the 'Son of France' Louis Joseph, Duc de Vendôme was ordered to assist him. In practice, neither Bourgogne nor Vendôme were in charge of

A French trumpeter and a kettle-drummer, as depicted in an early 18th-century engraving. Musicians like these were used to transmit orders to their fellow cavalrymen during the heat of battle, and to help bolster the morale of the troops. (Stratford Archive)

the army, as effective command was held jointly. This was a singularly unsatisfactory arrangement, as the skilled Vendôme was hindered by the inexperienced prince of the royal blood.

The two commanders disagreed from the start, with Vendôme wanting to strengthen the French defensive position by besieging Huy, and Bourgogne favouring an advance towards Brussels. They outnumbered Marlborough, who had only around 90,000 men at his disposal, and Bourgogne was convinced he would avoid a battle. Vendôme was unconvinced, but the Brussels plan was adopted, and the army marched out of its camp near Mons in late May. Marlborough was based outside Brussels, and he blocked the French advance by moving to Louvain and threatening the enemy's flank. By 2 June the French army was encamped at Braine-l'Alleud, near the site of the later battle of Waterloo.

The French remained there for a month, while Marlborough called for Imperial reinforcements, which would give his army parity of size with the French. They arrived on 7 July – a mixed force of 12,000 horse and foot, commanded by Prince Eugene. By then, however, the strategic picture had changed dramatically. The wily Vendôme had been planning a dramatic way to break the impasse, and on 4 July he made his move. Two fast-moving columns sped westwards from Braine-l'Alleud to secure the bridges over the river Dendre, and then push on to Ghent. The city fell to a *ruse de guerre* on 5 July, and Bruges fell two days later. Meanwhile, the main French army had broken camp and it marched west too. Once it crossed the Dendre, Bourgogne and Vendôme destroyed the bridges behind them. Marlborough had been wrong-footed – not only had the French stolen a march on him, but they had effectively reclaimed a large swathe of the Spanish Netherlands in the process.

Marlborough marched in pursuit. He passed through Brussels on 5 July and then headed south-west in an attempt to intercept the French as they crossed the Dendre. By then though the French had already crossed the river and were marching towards the river Scheldt. There were three main crossing points in that part of Flanders – at Ghent, Oudenarde and Tournai. Two of these three were in French hands, and by seizing Oudenarde Bourgogne and Vendôme would cut Marlborough off from the coast. On 10 July, when Marlborough was crossing the river Dendre at Lessines, the French were two days ahead of him, their troops approaching Oudenarde from the north. Marlborough pressed on by forced marches, but he sent Cadogan ahead with 11,000 men to provide whatever support he could to the garrison.

The French were at Gavere, on the eastern bank of the Scheldt, 6 miles (10km) north of Oudenarde itself. The scene was set for one of the most unusual battles of the war – a meeting engagement, where both sides fed troops into the fight as the day wore on. The fate of Ghent, Oudenarde and all the cities in western Flanders hung in the balance. Just as importantly, the military reputations of Marlborough and Vendôme were at stake.

The battle of Oudenarde

In the days before the battle Marlborough had marched his army more than 50 miles (80km) in 60 hours, a feat which allowed him to reach Oudenarde at roughly the same time as the French. The speed of Marlborough's march was helped by good staffwork – he had bread baked for his men, he prepared the crossings at Lessines before his main body arrived and he used Cadogan to scout ahead, identify and prepare good camping grounds. They were also looking for any signs of the French. As dawn broke on the morning of 11 July, Bourgogne and Vendôme at Gavere were unable to agree on a plan. They were unsure where Marlborough was, but they knew Cadogan was close by and that they outnumbered him. Bourgogne wanted to avoid battle, while Vendôme wanted to attack Cadogan. As the French army was stirring, Cadogan entered Oudenarde and supervised the construction of pontoon bridges just beyond the northern outskirts of the city. They were there to speed Marlborough's move over onto the west bank.

At 10.00am the French began crossing over the river Scheldt at Gavere, and an advance guard was sent south to seize the high ground to the north of Oudenarde. As Marlborough force-marched his infantry, 40 squadrons of his cavalry surged ahead to support Cadogan. These cavalry encountered the French advance guard a little after 1.00pm, near the village of Eine, 2 miles (3km) downstream from Oudenarde. The French commander, the Duc de Biron, who commanded the advance guard, spotted the dust clouds raised by Marlborough's army approaching Oudenarde. His report was met with disbelief. 'If they are there, the Devil must have carried them – such marching is impossible' declared Vendôme. He still thought he was facing Cadogan, and had already sent the army southwards. A major battle was now inevitable – the only question was whether one side or the other would reach the battlefield first, and so overwhelm their opponent's advance guard before the rest of their opponent's army could arrive.

The battlefield of Oudenarde was bounded to the east by the river Scheldt. Gently rising ground sloped upwards from Oudenarde towards the north. Three small streams ran in a roughly easterly direction across the battlefield

The battle of Oudenarde, 11 July 1708

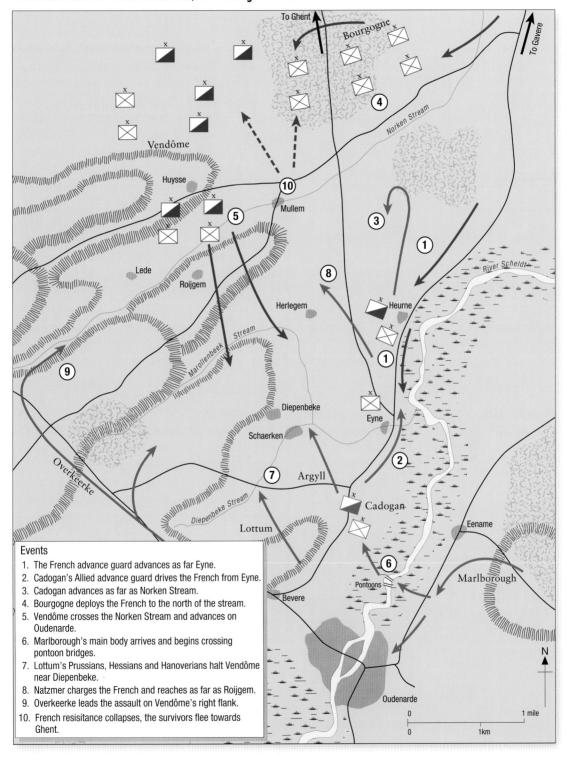

Events

1. The French advance guard advances as far Eyne.
2. Cadogan's Allied advance guard drives the French from Eyne.
3. Cadogan advances as far as Norken Stream.
4. Bourgogne deploys the French to the north of the stream.
5. Vendôme crosses the Norken Stream and advances on Oudenarde.
6. Marlborough's main body arrives and begins crossing pontoon bridges.
7. Lottum's Prussians, Hessians and Hanoverians halt Vendôme near Diepenbeke.
8. Natzmer charges the French and reaches as far as Roijgem.
9. Overkeerke leads the assault on Vendôme's right flank.
10. French resisitance collapses, the survivors flee towards Ghent.

Three sergeants of foot wearing French-style military dress, as depicted in a Bavarian military manual, published in 1723. By the early 18th century the partisan shown here had become a badge of rank rather than a weapon. (Bayerische Staatsbibliothek, Munich)

before debouching into the Scheldt. The Norken to the north marked the northern boundary of the arena, while two smaller streams – the Marollenbeek and the Diepenbeke – lay farther south, closer to Oudenarde. Several small hamlets were scattered throughout the area, which was further divided by fields, copses, hedges, tracks and orchards. The banks of the Scheldt were marshy, but the ground farther inland was firm, dry and pastoral.

The battle was a confused affair, as could be expected from a meeting engagement, but in general terms the French reinforced their advance guard from the north, while the Allies approached Cadogan's troops from the south, through Oudenarde or over the pontoon bridges. Cadogan concentrated his troops on the east, near the Scheldt, which marked the Allied right flank. Reinforcements from both sides extended the lines to the west, with the French on the left commanded by the Duc de Bourgogne, while Marshal Vendôme took charge of the centre and right. The 'Son of France' remained on the defensive, passively resisting Cadogan's attempts to drive him back towards the north.

For his part Marshal Vendôme occupied the high ground farther to the west, and then advanced forward, extending his line as reinforcements arrived. As a result of his co-commander's passivity he and his men bore the brunt of the fighting, and he soon discovered that the Allies were able to feed men into the fight faster than the French. While both armies had around 80,000–85,000 men on the battlefield, the French lacked the experienced staff officers needed to funnel these troops where they were needed most. Consequently the Allies enjoyed local superiority in numbers where it mattered. For instance, Cadogan's cavalry, supported by the Duke of Argyll's foot, were able to push General Biron's advance guard back from Eine, overwhelming a brigade of Swiss troops before being halted in front of the Norken stream by Bourgogne's main army.

Bourgogne then briefly went over to the attack, sending cavalry forward over the stream, which clashed with their Prussian counterparts near the village of Huerne. The French then withdrew, covered by infantry ordered forward by Vendôme, and Bourgogne withdrew to his command post beside the windmill at Roijgem, south of Huise, on the south bank of the Norken. It was almost as if he had lost interest in the battle. More likely he felt out of his depth. It was now around 4.30pm. Vendôme took charge, launching attacks against the Allies who by now had reached the line of the Marollenbeek stream. As the battle subsided on the Allied right the fighting grew in intensity in the centre, as both sides reinforced the brigades in the front line. What could have tipped the battle in the French favour at this point was the intervention of Bourgogne, and the 30,000 men he held back behind the Norken.

By 5.30pm Vendôme had around 25,000 men under his direct command in the centre, and was pushing forward, threatening Cadogan's left flank. The French cavalry were in reserve, waiting for the order to attack. Fortunately for Marlborough, the Prussian Count Lottum arrived at the head of 20 battalions of foot, and the French were held. At 6.00pm Marlborough handed control of the right wing to Prince Eugene and joined Lottum on the banks of the Diepenbeke stream. Marlborough saw the open left flank as the key to victory, especially as it offered a way to concentrate his forces against Vendôme. He diverted 18 battalions of Hanovarian and Hessian troops to the Diepenbeke, who massed behind Lottum's Prussians. He also repeated his trick of Ramillies, ordering Lottum to leave his colour parties where they were in the centre and concentrate his men on the right flank, which boosted Eugene's command to around 30,000 men. What he planned was a double encirclement, with the aim of trapping Vendôme's wing between the Norken and the Diepenbeke.

At this stage the Dutch were arriving on the field, led by Count Ouwerkerk. Marlborough ordered him to march them round the exposed right flank of the French army, then to attack them from the west. To distract the French, he ordered Eugene to unleash his cavalry, attacking north-west, towards Bourgogne's command post at Roijgem, just behind Vendôme's centre. The cavalry attack was launched a little after 6.30pm, spearheaded by General Natzmer and his Prussian horse. They scattered the waiting lines of French horse, only to be stopped short of Roijgem Mill by the Maison du Roi. At 7.00pm Marlborough also sent the Hanovarians and Hessians into the fray, pinning Vendôme's infantry in place behind Diepenbeke village. Finally, at 7.30pm, the Dutch were in position. This was Marlborough's battle-winning moment.

The attack was a spectacular success. The French appeared to have been taken completely by surprise, and while Vendôme tried to transfer his reserves to meet this new threat from his right flank, this wasn't enough to stop the Dutch. They swept on, until the French line resembled a 'U', with its apex near the hamlet of Diepenbeke and its rear near the mill at Roijgem. This area of course was still being contested by Eugene's cavalry, who had now been reinforced by infantrymen. In effect Vendôme's men were caught in a pocket, about 1½ miles (2.5km) deep and a mile (1.5km) wide. The French were now in complete disarray, and their resolve was collapsing. The only question now was whether the Dutch could seal them into a pocket before nightfall.

At 9.00pm the two French commanders met each other near Huise. This was the first time they had spoken directly to each other since the battle began. Even at that late moment an all-out attack by Bourgogne's left wing would probably have forced Prince Eugene to pull back, and so allow the rest of the French army to reach safety. Instead the 'Son of France' proposed an immediate retreat to Ghent – a suggestion which was vigorously opposed by Vendôme. What saved the French was rain. A heavy downpour began around 9.30pm, just as darkness fell. Firing slackened and stopped, and Allied units halted in the darkness rather than risk blundering into the enemy unawares. As a result the French in the pocket managed to escape, withdrawing in

LILLE.

In August 1708 Marlborough laid siege to the great French fortified city of Lille – the cornerstone of France's barrier of fortresses. Thanks to the efforts of Marshal Boufflers, it took Marlborough the rest of the campaigning season to capture the city. (Stratford Archive)

bedraggled and weary columns over the Norken stream, close to the windmill of Roijgem. Eventually, Marlborough called off any attempt at a pursuit, and the Allies waited until morning to gauge the scale of their victory.

While Oudenarde wasn't a spectacular triumph like Blenheim or Ramillies, it was still an impressive victory. The official Allied casualty list came to just over 800 men killed and 2,100 wounded. The French losses are harder to gauge, as both sides claimed widely differing figures. The official French line was that they lost no more than 7,000 men killed or wounded – a similar total to the Allies. A further 1,800 men were taken prisoner in the pocket. According to the Allies they captured around 7,000 prisoners, a total which can be verified by Allied provisioning records. Whatever the exact total, the French suffered a serious defeat – not a mortal one, but one that demoralized their army and allowed Marlborough to dictate the pace of the rest of the season's campaign.

The French withdrew to Ghent, as the Allies blocked any direct line of retreat towards the safety of Lille or Tournai. While Ghent would remain in French hands for a few more months, it was obvious that the French stood to lose their recent gains in western Flanders. The Allies moved south to Ypres and set to destroying the western end of the French defensive lines. Marlborough then advocated an advance down the coast, but the Dutch government vetoed any plan that left Holland exposed. Instead, Marlborough opted for the capture of Lille, the strongest Vauban fortified city in the region. The capture of Lille would establish Marlborough in France itself.

The French were already recovering from their blow at Oudenarde. The Duke of Berwick was sent to Flanders with reinforcements from the Rhine, while the ageing Marshal Boufflers reinforced Lille and flooded the surrounding countryside to impede Marlborough. Prince Eugene and 35,000 men laid siege to the city on 14 August, while Marlborough commanded the 75,000-strong covering force. The French under Berwick moved in from the west as if to attack Marlborough, but in the end they kept their distance, apart from sparring with an Allied supply column at Wyendael on 27 September, and attempting to run supplies through Eugene's siege lines a few weeks later. The one thing they were unwilling to do was to risk another battle with Marlborough. Consequently, Marshal Boufflers was forced to surrender Lille on 25 October, though the citadel held out for another six weeks.

While the siege was drawing to a climax, the elector of Bavaria tried to distract Marlborough by attempting a raid on Brussels. Striking north from Mons, he reached the outskirts of the city on 22 November but lacked the artillery needed to breach its defences. Marlborough simply needed to threaten to cut his line of retreat in order to make the elector retreat again. Vendôme's army evacuated Ghent and Bruges in late December and retired to Dunkirk. Both cities were recaptured by the Allies, wiping out the last French gains of the year. Louis XIV tried to put a brave face on it, but in effect Marlborough had bundled his armies out of all of Flanders save Tournai and Mons; he had captured the great fortress of Lille, and he was poised to take the fight into France the following year. That winter Louis had very little reason to be cheerful.

Malplaquet

Sparring around Mons

The winter of 1708–09 was one of the worst in living memory, and in France this killed off crops, resulting in widespread famine. While Louis wanted peace, the Allies were unwilling to agree on anything other than the most draconian terms, increasing their demands at each peace talk. In the end the French abandoned the process and the war continued. The year 1709 also marked a turning point. The war was entering its final phase, and the string of Marlborough's victories was coming to an end. War weariness was setting in on all sides. Louis' treasury was exhausted, but the French increasingly saw no way out, apart from fighting hard to achieve a better deal.

In Flanders, Marshal Vendôme was replaced by Marshal Villars, who still enjoyed considerable respect as a commander. His first task was to feed his army. It was short of food, so famine or not Villars simply sent troops to requisition what he needed. The army still struggled to survive during the winter, and Villars also had the problem of establishing a new defensive line. With Lille lost, the French established a line that ran from Ypres to Tournai, forming a wide loop around Lille on the way. It then ran south-east to Mons before reaching the river Sambre above Maubeuge. From there it ran downstream to Namur. Villars was busy – garrisons were strengthened, defences were rebuilt and the manpower losses of 1708 were made good. He also began work on a new defensive line some 20 miles (32km) to the rear, stretching between Aire on the river Lys and the town of Douai.

The formidable defences of Tournai were built by Vauban in the late 17th century, who reinforced and strengthened the medieval walls, then augmented them by adding a system of bastions and outworks. (Courtesy of Brig. Charles S. Grant)

Marlborough still enjoyed the assistance of Prince Eugene of Savoy in 1709, and the two commanders devised a plan of campaign that would appease the conservative Dutch while still breaching this new French defensive line. It began with an attack on Tournai, which was besieged on 27 June. The town had substantial defences, and the French expected that the siege would drag on for most of the year. This time Marlborough supervised the siege,

while Eugene provided the covering force, charged with keeping the French army at bay. The town itself surrendered after a month, but its garrison withdrew into the citadel, where they held out until 3 September. In the meantime Villars had strengthened his other garrisons and improved and extended his fallback line, now called the Lines of Cambrin, which now ran on from Douai to Valenciennes, where it joined the existing line of defences on the river Sambre at Maubeuge, after running through Condé and Bavai.

Marlborough now moved eastwards to Mons, the capture of which would compromise what remained of Villars' forward line and force him to withdraw to the unfinished lines farther south. Villars responded by moving his army forward, occupying a position midway between Mons and Valenciennes. He arrived there on 7 September, the day after Marlborough began the siege of Mons. His plan was to move closer in order to prevent the Allies from investing the city, but he was too late – the Allied army had already surrounded the place. Villars was a cautious commander; after all, the French had few reserves left, and his army was all that stood between Marlborough and Paris. He was camped near the Bois de Boussu, one of a number of large woods or forests that ran in a line from Boussu on the river Haine south-east towards Maubeuge, on the river Sambre. Eugene was encamped to the east of the wood, while Marlborough was occupied around Mons.

The battle of Malplaquet

On 9 September Marshal Villars marched his army down the line of woods screening Mons, keeping to the French side of them. He halted when he reached the small village of Malplaquet, 3 miles (5km) north of the French town of Bavai. There he took up position between two of the woods – the Bois de Sars on his left and the Bois de Lanières on his right. As soon as he arrived on 10 September he set his men to work digging field fortifications which stretched between the two large woods, spanning the 'Gap of Malplaquet'.

Redoubts studded the line, and overlapping fields of fire were established to cover the centre, where Villars expected Marlborough to attempt his main assault. This was French field engineering at its very best. He even threw up fieldworks in the woods themselves, in case Marlborough or Eugene tried to turn his flank. Villars had around 75,000 men under his command, supported by 80 pieces of artillery. Marshal Boufflers commanded the right, General d'Artagnan the left, while General de Guiche held the centre. Villars held his cavalry and guard in reserve. In fact he did everything to ensure that for Marlborough, this was going to be no easy victory.

When Marlborough learned of Villars' approach he had little option but to raise the siege, recall Eugene, and march south to meet Villars at Malplaquet. Marlborough's army approached the French lines during the afternoon of 10 September, and, while his troops assembled, Marlborough decided just how to attack Villars' formidable defensive position. Clearly there was no easy way to outflank it, although he had already ordered a small column of horse and foot under General Withers to find a way round

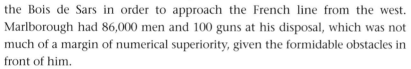

the Bois de Sars in order to approach the French line from the west. Marlborough had 86,000 men and 100 guns at his disposal, which was not much of a margin of numerical superiority, given the formidable obstacles in front of him.

In the end, Marlborough opted for a variant of his standard plan of attack – assaulting the two flanks first, and then launching a knockout blow against the centre once the enemy had stripped it of troops. The question was, would the French fall for the same trick again? Generals Schulenburg and Lottum, under Eugene, would hack their way through the defences of the Bois de Sars on the Allied right, and the Prince of Orange, commanding Dutch troops, would attack the French left. The French would almost certainly strip their centre to support their flanks, at which point the Earl of Orkney would be unleashed at the head of a force of British and Hanovarian troops, with orders to capture the redoubts guarding the French centre. The Allied cavalry would then pass through the line of redoubts and charge the French cavalry beyond. The plan would work, as long as Villars and Boufflers reacted as Marlborough expected them to. It would be a tough fight – the hardest yet – but Marlborough had confidence in his troops, and knew he could rely on them.

The Allied guns began their bombardment at around 8.00am, and then Eugene's 58 infantry battalions began their advance towards the French waiting in the Bois de Sars. The fighting was fierce and bloody, with Schulenburg attacking from the front while Lottum assaulted the French from the flank. Both attacks ran into formidable defences, and French light guns poured canister shot into the advancing Imperial, Prussian and other German troops. Half an hour later the Prince of Orange launched his own attack, as

In this tapestry of the battle of Malplaquet, Marlborough enjoys a commanding view of the battlefield. In fact the terrain was virtually flat, and the battlefield was broken by dense woods, making it exceptionally difficult to control the course of events. (Stratford Archive)

30 battalions of Dutch infantry advanced against the French right. There, the French line doubled back on itself to conform to a shallow gully formed by a track; the Dutch infantry attacking d'Artagnan's men on the extreme French right suddenly found themselves enfiladed by a 20-gun battery, hidden by the curve in the French line and by the dip in the ground. The attacking lines were shredded, and the Dutch had little option but to retire. Some 5,000 Dutch troops fell in less than half an hour, and the ground there was carpeted with the dead and dying.

The Prince of Orange re-formed his lines and attacked again, protected by the Allied cavalry ranged behind him. This second attack, launched at around 9.15am, fared no better and was repulsed with heavy losses. The Dutch were preparing to launch a third attack with the survivors when orders came from Marlborough to go over onto the defensive. He wasn't prepared to waste any more lives on what was essentially a diversion from the main assault. By that

The battle of Malplaquet, 11 September 1709

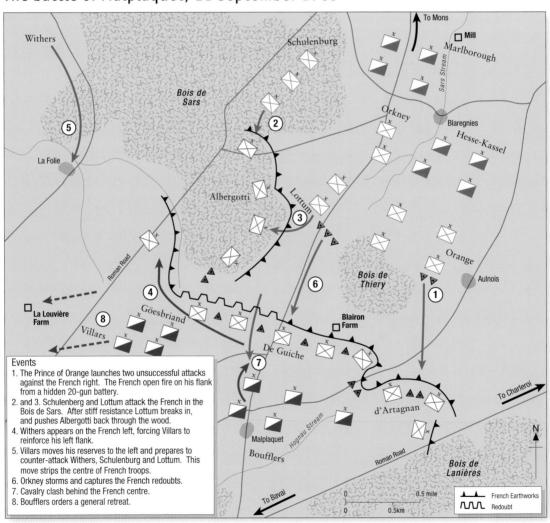

Events
1. The Prince of Orange launches two unsuccessful attacks against the French right. The French open fire on his flank from a hidden 20-gun battery.
2. and 3. Schulenberg and Lottum attack the French in the Bois de Sars. After stiff resistance Lottum breaks in, and pushes Albergotti back through the wood.
4. Withers appears on the French left, forcing Villars to reinforce his left flank.
5. Villars moves his reserves to the left and prepares to counter-attack Withers, Schulenburg and Lottum. This move strips the centre of French troops.
6. Orkney storms and captures the French redoubts.
7. Cavalry clash behind the French centre.
8. Boufflers orders a general retreat.

British troops clearing away the enemy defences lining the edge of the Bois de Sars near Malplaquet, while their comrades drive the French back through the wood. In fact this assault was carried out by German rather than British troops. (Stratford Archive)

time the attack on the Bois de Sars had stalled too. Although Eugene's men had cleared the defences, French reinforcements had been brought up, and they manned a second line of defences, on the edge of the forest.

Despite these bloody setbacks, Marlborough's plan was working. To halt Eugene, Villars had ordered 17 battalions to move from his centre to his left to form the second line of defence the Allies now faced. Another threat was posed by General Withers, whose column of 19 battalions and 10 squadrons merged on the southern side of the Bois de Sars, immediately behind the French left flank. More reserves had to be moved to face these new Allied troops, until no fewer than 50 battalions were grouped on the French left flank. Worse, they lacked an overall commander, as at around noon Villars was wounded and carried from the field. His reinforcement of his left flank meant that his centre was very sparsely defended. Marlborough, of course, had been waiting for this moment. At 11.45am he ordered the Earl of Orkney to advance, and his 15 battalions headed straight down the line of the Mons to Malplaquet road, towards the enemy redoubts.

The battlefield of Malplaquet looking west from the Mons–Bavai road towards what remains of the Bois de Sars. This marked the salient of the French line, which was attacked by Prince Eugene. (Courtesy of Brig. Charles S. Grant)

Orkney's men stormed the redoubts, ignoring the French fire, to sweep over and through the defences. With these five bastions in Allied hands, Marlborough could send in his cavalry. This would be the climax of the battle – 30,000 Allied horsemen surged forward and passed Orkney's cheering men. The French cavalry – some 20,000 of them – were waiting for them.

The battlefield of Malplaquet looking east from the monument towards Blairon Farm and the Bois de Thiery. This was where Orkney's artillery was sited, and where his reserves waited for the order to attack. (Courtesy of Brig. Charles S. Grant)

A great cavalry clash ensued as both sides charged, counter-charged, wheeled, retired and charged again in a swirling mass of dust and horses. Marshal Boufflers was now in command of the French army, and while he threw in what cavalry reserves he could, it was clear that the French horsemen were badly outnumbered. The French were gradually driven back towards the outskirts of Malplaquet, and by 2.00pm it was clear that the battle was lost.

Unlike previous battles though, the French withdrew in good order. The troops on the French right had lost very few men during the battle, and they retired down the old Roman road leading to Bavai in a textbook withdrawal. The troops on the French left withdrew too, but they had a harder job disengaging from the Allies. Nevertheless, by 3.00pm they had broken contact, and were also withdrawing towards Bavai, taking most of their guns with them. What remained of the French cavalry covered their retreat. While this was an Allied victory, it wasn't a decisive one, and for once the French had performed superbly. As Marlborough himself put it in a letter written that evening: 'The French have defended themselves better in this action than in any battle I have seen.'

The cost of Marlborough's victory at Malplaquet was extremely high. The Allies had lost around 21,000 men killed and wounded that day, which was roughly a quarter of Marlborough's entire army. The French lost roughly half that – 11,000 men, while a further 500 were taken prisoner. It was enough for the French to claim a victory of sorts. Villars even wrote to Louis XIV, writing: 'Your Majesty's troops have done marvels. Although your army is in retreat it will become clear that it lost less men than the enemy.' It was certainly the bloodiest battle of the entire war, and the most costly fought in Europe for another half century. Marlborough had won, but it was a pyrrhic victory, and it lost him the support of the rulers and politicians whose troops made up the core of his army. Although nobody knew it at the time, Malplaquet would be Marlborough's last battle.

After the bloodletting

Mons surrendered just over five weeks later, which effectively brought this bruising campaign to an end. Marlborough was still convinced that his costly victory was enough of a blow to force Louis XIV to negotiate a peace. Instead, the French seemed to rally. After Malplaquet they knew they were defending France itself, and the last reserves of money, men and provisions were given to Marshal Villars, who continued to enjoy the trust of the King. The negotiations petered out, and campaigning began afresh in 1710. By that time, though, both sides seemed unwilling to risk another bloodletting. Marlborough captured the fortress of Douai on 25 June, and Béthume on 28 August. A final town – Aire – fell to Marlborough on 8 November. While the loss of these three fortresses meant that the latest French defensive line had to be pushed back even farther, there always seemed to be another line of forts immediately behind them.

More peace talks the following winter also came to nothing, but by that time it was clear that Marlborough's days as the Allied commander-in-chief were numbered. Before Blenheim he had courted the Whig party, as his friend Sidney Godolphin advised him that he needed their political support. By 1706 though, Godolphin had lost the trust of Queen Anne, and the Whig ascendancy in Parliament also met with her disapproval. Marlborough was now associated with the Whigs, and so the support he enjoyed from the Queen also began to wane. This was mirrored in the Queen's relationship with Duchess Sarah. While Sarah had once been the confidante of Queen Anne, cracks appeared in their close relationship, and Sarah too began to drift out of royal favour.

By 1708 Sarah and the Queen had fallen out altogether, and Marlborough's meetings with his sovereign became increasingly strained. Marlborough supported the Whig view that the war should continue until a favourable peace could be found – the slogan 'no peace without Spain' highlighted their demand that Louis renounce all dynastic claims to the Spanish throne. Queen Anne was increasingly open to more moderate views. While Marlborough's battlefield successes were enough to keep the critics at bay, the bloodbath of Malplaquet gave the moderates the excuse they needed to step up their campaign.

The Tories might have been in opposition, but when Marlborough returned to England in the winter of 1709–10 they roundly criticized him for the loss of life and his refusal to consider an immediate peace. His detractors even claimed that he attended peace talks only to sabotage them. When the 1710

The Malplaquet Monument in the centre of the battlefield commemorates the two French marshals who faced Marlborough on the battlefield, rather than the British commander who defeated them and won his last blood-soaked victory there. (Courtesy of Brig. Charles S. Grant)

The grim aftermath of battle, as depicted in Joseph Leopold's *Les Excercises de Mars*, a Franco-German military manual dated 1700. Looters strip the bodies of their clothing and possessions, while a priest administers the last rites to a dying soldier. (Stratford Archive)

campaign ended he visited the Queen again, and in January 1711 he learned that her relationship with Sarah was now irrevocably damaged. She purposely refused to name him as Captain-General for life – a political more than a military snub, which sent a signal to his detractors that he had effectively lost the support of the Queen. In 1711 he returned to Flanders for what would be his last campaign. The French had built a new defensive line, named Ne Plus Ultra (No Farther). To Marlborough this was the perfect challenge. It ran from Arras to Cambrai and Valenciennes, then linked up with the existing defensive lines at the river Sambre.

In the end Marlborough breached these lines whilst losing almost no casualties. Marlborough feinted elsewhere to distract Marshal Villars, and then on 6 July he stormed and captured Arleux, near Arras. Marlborough retired again, and the French retook the town, but the defences had been razed. In effect it created a breach in the Ne Plus Ultra line. Marlborough moved to the west to the countryside around Denain, and Villars followed. At that point Marlborough doubled back and crossed the lines at Arleux, which was virtually undefended. It was a magnificent piece of manoeuvring.

Marlborough went on to besiege Bouchain, halfway between Valenciennes and Cambrai, which fell on 12 September. The Ne Plus Ultra line had been breached in only three months, and all that was left of the great string of Vauban fortifications between Marlborough and Paris were Arras, Cambria and Le Quesnoy. Marlborough could take these the following year, and then there would be nothing Louis XIV could do but make peace on whatever terms the Allies chose to dictate. Unfortunately for Marlborough, the capture of Bouchain marked the end of his last campaign.

Unknown to Marlborough, the Whig government had opened secret peace negotiations with the French, and talks had been taking place while Marlborough was carving his way through Northern France. Robert Harley had

Earl of Orkney's advance at Malplaquet

Marlborough's plan at Malplaquet was similar to those that had brought success at Blenheim and Ramillies. He launched attacks against the enemy flanks, hoping the French would strip their centre of troops to reinforce their threatened line. At the critical moment he would unleash his reserves against the French centre, hoping to achieve a decisive breakthrough. At Malplaquet this reserve consisted of 15 battalions of British and Hanovarian infantry, under the command of the Earl of Orkney. These men had to endure intermittent French fire for most of the morning, but at 11.45am Marlborough finally ordered Orkney to advance, and his infantry advanced steadily, succeeding in driving the French from the redoubts that marked the enemy line. The way was now clear for the Allied cavalry, who passed the redoubts to engage their French counterparts. Eventually, numbers began to tell, and by 2.00pm the French retired from the field. In this spirited scene Orkney's British infantry – Scottish soldiers of Orkney's own Royal Regiment – have just begun their steady advance towards the waiting French. In Marlborough's time a British battalion of around 500 men was deployed in three ranks, allowing the whole battalion to fire their muskets at the enemy.

Marlborough at the Siege of Bouchain, 1711. Marshal Villars elected to avoid battle, and sacrificed the town rather than risk suffering another defeat at the hands of Marlborough. The capture of the city of Bouchain on 12 September was Marlborough's last military triumph. (Stratford Archive)

convinced the Queen that peace was essential. In early December 1711 she announced as much, which Marlborough took as a deliberate slight. He remained the greatest obstacle to a negotiated peace, and so Harley set out to blacken his name, concocting charges of fraud and mismanagement. On 29 December Queen Anne used these trumped-up charges as an excuse to dismiss Marlborough. The general who had given her a string of victories, and had brought France to the brink of total defeat, was sacked, almost without a second thought. He was succeeded by the Duke of Ormonde, who would essentially supervise the withdrawal of British troops from the Continent. The war would drag on for two more years, and Villars would enjoy renewed successes against less capable opponents. For Marlborough, this was the ultimate betrayal, the sacrifice of victory on the altar of party politics and court intrigue. It was a shabby end to a sparkling career.

OPPOSING COMMANDERS

During his career John Churchill, Duke of Marlborough, pitted his skills against no fewer than ten leading military commanders, the majority of whom were marshals of France. Until their defeat at his hands they were considered some of the most highly respected generals of their day. Here is the impressive roll-call of the rivals Churchill vanquished.

James Scott, Duke of Monmouth (1649–85)

James, Duke of Monmouth, the illegitimate eldest son of King Charles II, first saw action as a teenager serving alongside his uncle, James, Duke of York. He was rewarded with command of a troop of Life Guards, and became the colonel of the regiment at the age of 20. The following year he was named as the Captain-General of the English Army, a ludicrous promotion for one so young. Still, he showed military promise – during the third Anglo-Dutch War (1672–74) he commanded an English brigade fighting alongside the French, and distinguished himself at the Siege of Maastricht (1673). He formed a close bond with the young John Churchill, declaring that the future Duke of Marlborough had saved his life. Further active commands followed, and he saw action against the French (1678) and against Scottish religious rebels – the Covenanters (1679). However, he is best remembered for his rebellion against his uncle James II and VII, which ended in disaster at the battle of Sedgemoor (1685). There he was outfought by his old comrade John Churchill, and ultimately Monmouth paid for his mistakes with his life. He should be regarded as an inspiring figure, but only a competent general.

Louis de Crévant, Duc d'Humières, marshal of France (1628–94)

By the time the Duc d'Humières encountered the Earl of Marlborough on the battlefield of Walcourt in 1689, the veteran marshal of France was over 60 years old, and in failing health. He commanded a brigade at the battle of the Dunes (1658), and during the intervening three decades he served France well, participating in several major battles and sieges during the Dutch Wars (1672–78 and 1683–84) and the War of the Grand Alliance (1688–97). He became a marshal of France in 1688 and took command of the French army in Flanders the following year. It was there that he met defeat at the hands of the Prince of Waldeck, who was ably assisted by Marlborough. D'Humières was an above-average commander, but he was one of the few French generals to experience defeat during the War of the Grand Alliance.

Louis de France, Duc de Bourgogne (1682–1712)

The eldest son of Louis, the Dauphin of France, Louis, Duc de Bourgogne, was the grandson of Louis XIV. He was therefore a 'Son of France', the title given to those who were the son or grandson of the French king, and consequently a leading prince of the royal blood. Bourgogne had no military experience of any note before his grandfather gave him command of the French army in Flanders. However, since 1702 he had served on the High Council, which advised the King on matters of military strategy and diplomacy. That at least should have given him some grounding in the problems of military command. This lack of experience meant that when he was given command of the army in Flanders he was advised by the far-more-experienced Duc de Vendôme. Unfortunately for them, Bourgogne frequently ignored this advice, and chose his own course of action. His inexperience and lack of aggression played a major part in his defeat at the battle of Oudenarde (1708), and even with Vendôme's help he was no match for Marlborough and Eugene.

Louis François, Duc de Boufflers, marshal of France (1644–1711)

When he and Villars faced Marlborough and Eugene at the battle of Malplaquet (1709), Marshal Boufflers was one of the most experienced soldiers in the French Army, and one of the oldest. He first saw action in 1663, some 45 years before, and commanded a dragoon regiment six years later. He commanded a brigade during the Dutch War of 1672–78 and ended the war as maréchal de camp, a general of field rank. Further promotion and distinction followed, and in 1692 he became a marshal of France. After the defeat at Oudenarde in 1708 Boufflers took command of the key city of Lille, and, while he was eventually forced to surrender, he was commended for his

Louis-François, Duc de Boufflers (1644–1711), marshal of France, held Lille against Marlborough in 1708, and the following year he took command of the army at Malplaquet after Villars was wounded. He was competent but uninspired, and no match for Marlborough. (Stratford Archive)

leadership and fighting spirit. In 1709 he offered his services to Marshal Villars, and effectively became his deputy during the battle of Malplaquet. His performance during the battle was impressive – he held his wing with ease, and led the army in a skilfully executed fighting retreat after Villars was wounded. Marshal Boufflers should therefore be rated as one of Marlborough's more successful opponents.

Ferdinand, Compte de Marsin, marshal of France (1656–1706)

Marshal Marsin had a reputation as a practical commander and a soldier's general. He displayed great skill and bravery during the War of the Grand Alliance (1688–97), and became France's youngest lieutenant-general in 1693 and the Director General of Cavalry two years later. He played an important part in the battle of Neerwinden (1693), and ended the war with a good reputation as a field commander. He was also a diplomat, and acted as Louis XIV's ambassador in Spain during the vital negotiations that led to the coronation of Philip V. When the war began he was still in Spain, but in 1702 he was sent to Italy, where he fought under the Duc de Vendôme at the battle of Luzarra (1702). The following year he was sent to the Rhine, where he proved an able assistant to Marshal Tallard, helping to defeat the Imperialists at Speyerbach (1703). He was made a marshal of France by way of reward, but while a competent subordinate, Marsin proved a mediocre army commander. After Blenheim he returned to his subordinate role, and was killed during the Siege of Toulon two years after his defeat at Blenheim.

Maximilian II Emmanuel, the elector of Bavaria (r. 1679–1726), as depicted by Joseph Vivien in 1706. His alliance with the French proved a disaster for Bavaria, which was ravaged and occupied as a result of his policies. (Residenz, Munich)

Maximilian Emanuel II von Wittelsbach, elector of Bavaria (1662–1726)

The elector of Bavaria had some military experience before the War of the Spanish Succession, having fought against the Ottoman Turks in the 1680s. His decision to side with France rather than the Holy Roman Empire was surprising, especially as his wife was the daughter of the Austrian Emperor. It was certainly a decision he would come to regret. In 1702 he commanded his small Bavarian army in person, and in March 1703 he defeated an Imperialist army at the battle of Sieghardin. This, however, was his only battlefield success as an independent commander, athough he was present when Marshal Villars defeated the Imperialists at Höchstädt in September 1703. During the Blenheim campaign he needlessly dispersed his army to protect his own estates, and while his performance at Blenheim was adequate, it was uninspiring, as he appeared to make few command decisions once the battle had begun. After Blenheim he continued to fight alongside his French allies in the Spanish Netherlands, and should be rated as an average albeit unimaginative commander.

Camille d'Hostun, Duc de Tallard, marshal of France (1652–1728)

An experienced soldier, Marshal Tallard had served with distinction during the War of the Grand Alliance (1688–97), and became a lieutenant-general in 1693. He was appointed the French ambassador at the court of William III and II after the war, but was recalled to France in 1701 when hostilities resumed. He was described as short-sighted, nondescript and a lover of comfort, although he was also an above-average general, who managed to outmanoeuvre Eugene of Savoy on the Rhine in 1704 but allowed himself to be surprised and outwitted by Marlborough at Blenheim. After his capture on the battlefield he spent seven years in England as a prisoner, before being allowed to return to France in 1712.

François de Neufville, Duc de Villeroi, marshal of France (1644–1730)

Since childhood, Villeroi was a member of Louis XIV's inner circle of friends and advisers. He was also a soldier, and first saw service during the Dutch Wars of the late 17th century. However, he never held a command of any note until he became a marshal of France in 1693, a promotion owing to royal patronage rather than martial ability. He commanded the French army in Flanders during the final years of the War of the Grand Alliance (1688–97), and while his performance was uninspiring, he managed to hold on to the significant French gains in the Spanish Netherlands until the war finally drew to a close. The War of the Spanish Succession (1701–14) began badly for Villeroi when he was defeated by Eugene at Chieri (1701) and then captured at Cremona (1702). He was soon released, and he returned to Flanders, where he eventually faced Marlborough at the battle of Ramillies (1706). His defeat was so spectacular that he never held a military command again. He should be rated as nothing more than an average commander, and an unlucky one.

Louis Joseph de Bourbon, Duc de Vendôme, marshal of France (1654–1712)

Marshal Vendôme was a great-grandson of King Henri IV of France, albeit through an illegitimate line. His aunt was the mother of Prince Eugene of Savoy, and like his cousin he excelled himself as a soldier. By the start of the War of the Grand Alliance Vendôme was a major-general, and he distinguished himself in Flanders and Italy before gaining his first independent command in Spain. He captured Barcelona in 1697, and was rewarded by being named a marshal of France. In 1702 he succeeded Villeroi as the commander of the French army in Italy, and he performed well there, defeating his cousin Eugene at Cassano in 1705. The following year he was sent to Flanders to repair the damage done by Villeroi's defeat at Ramillies. While Vendôme did well, he was superseded by the inexperienced Duc de Bourgogne, and the

Louis Joseph, Duc de Vendôme (1654–1712), marshal of France, proved a highly capable commander, but during the battle of Oudenarde has was hamstrung by his inexperienced royal co-commander Louis, Duc de Bourgogne. As a result he was outmanoeuvred by Marlborough. (Stratford Archive)

Claude, Duc de Villars (1653–1734), marshal of France, was the last of the French commanders to face Marlborough in the field. Of all of them, he was the one who came closest to defeating Marlborough on the battlefield of Malplaquet. (Stratford Archive)

two were defeated by Marlborough at Oudenarde in 1708. In 1711 he was sent to Spain, where he won two victories for Philip V before his sudden death on campaign. Marshal Vendôme was a skilled general, and probably one of the two opponents who gave Marlborough a real challenge.

Claude Louis Hector, Duc de Villars, marshal of France (1653–1734)

Marshal Villars first saw active service during the Dutch War of 1672–78, and won laurels at the siege of Maastricht (1673) and the battle of Seneffe (1674). He also won the distrust of the Marquis de Louvois, the French king's war minister, who blocked his promotion to high command until 1687. In the meantime, Villars served as a diplomat in the Bavarian court, and became a close friend of the elector of Bavaria. During the War of the Grand Alliance he served in Flanders, commanding the army's cavalry arm, and he gained a reputation as a skilled and conscientious field commander. During the opening rounds of the War of the Spanish Succession he defeated the Imperialists at Friedlingen (1702) and Höchstädt (1703), and as a result of these successes he became a marshal of France. In 1709 he was given command of the Army of Flanders, and while he was wounded and defeated at Malplaquet, he fought a skilful defensive battle and inflicted heavy casualties on Marlborough's army. He continued to exercise command of the army in Flanders, and after Marlborough's removal he inflicted a sound defeat on Eugene of Savoy at Denain (1712). His actions did much to save France and to help her diplomats negotiate an honourable peace. Of all of Marlborough's opponents, Marshal Villars was the most able, and the most popular with both his troops and the French people.

INSIDE THE MIND

What made Marlborough such a successful general? His military abilities speak for themselves. Here we are more concerned with his personality and character, and the traits that gave him such an edge over his opponents. For a start, his upbringing in genteel poverty had an impact on his personality, and may explain his parsimony in later life. Then there were the political tensions at home, with his father being a Royalist while his grandmother supported Parliament. This may have explained his reticence to speak his mind openly in later life, and why he displayed such self-control over his emotions. His education was basic – he never mastered the art of spelling – yet he became a master of the military craft and a copious correspondent. His critics may have singled him out as ambitious and ruthless, but the men under his command saw a different Marlborough – a commander who cared about his men, and did what he could to help them.

Captain Robert Parker shows us a little of Marlborough's ability when he described an incident during the siege of Bouchain (1711), when he was ordered to assault a strongly held outwork:

> We plainly saw that their entrenchment was a perfect bulwark, strong and lofty, and crowded with men and cannon pointed directly at us; yet did they not fire a shot great or small, reserving all for us, on our advancing up to them. We wished much that the Duke might take a nearer view of the thing: and yet we judged that he chose rather to continue on the other side, in order to observe the motions of the enemy on that side, while we were attacking them on this. But while I was musing, the Duke of Marlborough (ever watchful, ever right) rode up quite unattended and alone, and posted himself a little on the right of my company of grenadiers, from whence he had a fair view of the greater part of the enemy's works.
>
> It is quite impossible for me to express the joy, which the sight of this man gave me at this very critical moment. I was now well satisfied that he would not push the thing, unless he saw a strong probability of success; nor was this my notion alone; it was the sense of the whole army, both officer and soldier, British and foreigner. And indeed we had all the reason in the world for it; for he never led us on to any one action, that we did not succeed in. He stayed only three or four minutes, and then rode back. We were in pain for him while he stayed, lest the enemy might have discovered him, and fired at him; in which case they could not well have missed him.
>
> He had not been longer from us, than he stayed, when orders came to us to retire. It may be presumed we were not long about it, and as the corn we stood in was high, we slipped off undiscovered, and were a good way down the hill before they perceived that we were retiring; and then they let fly all their great and small shot after us: but as we were by this time under the brow of the hill, all their shot went over our heads, insomuch that there was not a single man of all the grenadiers hurt.

The Duke of Marlborough depicted planning the siege of Bouchain in September 1711, assisted by Major-General Armstrong. Marlborough's Chief of Engineers was a master of siegecraft, and together the two men masterminded the breach of France's barrier of frontier forts. (Stratford Archive)

It is a singular testimony to Marlborough's concern for his men – and their reciprocal faith in him. He was a soldier's general, whose very presence raised their spirits and gave them confidence. They nicknamed him 'Corporal John' as a mark of respect, to show that he was one of them. Even his critics recognized that he was different from other generals – a man set apart from the ordinary. Someone who was openly critical of Marlborough was Colonel Van Goslinga, an officer in the Dutch Army. Despite this, or possibly because of it, Marlborough still invited the colonel to share space on his cloak after the two officers exhausted themselves in pursuit of the French after Ramillies. After the war, Goslinga summarized his commander, stressing the good points with the bad:

His mind is keen and subtle, his judgement both clear and sound, his insight quick and deep, with an all-embracing knowledge of men which no false show of merit can deceive. He expresses himself well, and even his very bad French is agreeable: he has a harmonious voice, and as a speaker of his own language he is considered amongst the best. His address is most courteous, and while his handsome and well-graced countenance engages every one in his favour at first sight, his perfect manners and gentleness win over even those who start with a prejudice or grudge against him. He has courage as he has shown on more than one occasion: he is an experienced soldier, and plans a campaign to admiration.

So far his good qualities. Now for the weak points which I consider I have discovered in him. The Duke is a profound dissembler, all the more dangerous that his manner and his words give the impression of frankness itself. His ambition knows no bounds, and an avarice that I can only call sordid, guides his entire conduct. If he has courage – and of this there is no question, whatever may be said by those who envy or hate him – he certainly lacks that firmness of soul which makes the true Hero. Sometimes on the eve of an action, he is irresolute or worse; he will not face difficulties, and occasionally lets reverses cast him down: of this I could give several eye-witness accounts. Yet I saw nothing of the kind either at Ramillies or Malplaquet, so that it may be that some constitutional weakness, unfitting him to bear fatigue, has something to do with it. He is not a strict disciplinarian, and allows his men too much rein, who have occasionally indulged in frightful excesses. Moreover he lacks the precise knowledge of military detail which a Commander-in-Chief should possess. But these defects are light when balanced against the rare gifts of this truly great man.

Goslinga was a Dutch 'deputy-in-the-field', a sort of political commissar, who frequently clashed with Marlborough when he thought Marlborough's actions weren't in the interests of the Dutch Republic. Despite this, he obviously realized that Marlborough was a military commander who – despite his flaws – was a man touched by genius.

WHEN WAR IS DONE

When Marlborough was dismissed by the Queen in December 1711 he had been accused of corruption by Robert Harley, who had succeeded Godolphin as Lord Treasurer. Although Marlborough had the evidence he needed to refute the allegations, the Queen refused to hear his case. For years Marlborough and Godolphin had enjoyed the ear of the Queen, but by 1711 the ailing Godolphin had fallen from favour and Duchess Sarah had been replaced as the Queen's confidante by Abigail Masham, Harley's cousin. He used Abigail as a weapon in his political war of supremacy in Parliament and in court, and first Godolphin and then Marlborough fell victim to his wiles.

Marlborough was expected to retire to his magnificent, draughty and unfinished palace at Woodstock, but, sickened of Britain, he decided to go on a tour of Europe instead. There he was fêted by rulers and statesmen in the courts of the Continent, showered with honours, and even made a prince of the Holy Roman Empire. Sarah accompanied him, and was delighted by her husband's widespread popularity – in such contrast to his treatment at home in Britain. It was a necessary final lap of honour, which helped take some of the sting out of his shabby treatment at home. Marlborough even visited his new Bavarian estates at Mindelheim, a gift from a grateful Emperor.

He also kept up his extensive network of contacts, and he remained well informed on the progress of the war and the peace negotiations, as well as the intrigues of the British court. Encouraged by Robert Harley – now the Earl of Oxford – the British and the Dutch had entered into peace talks, and a peace treaty was finally signed in Utrecht in April 1713. The Emperor and most of the German princes refused to have anything to do with the treaty, and they – including the elector of Hanover – continued the war for another year in an attempt to undermine the French. Marlborough also knew that the health of Queen Anne was failing. She had remained childless, and Marlborough favoured a transition of power to another Protestant dynasty – the House of Hanover. He lent his considerable diplomatic powers to ensure that this smooth line of succession would become a reality.

Strangely enough, he still maintained a correspondence with the Queen. When his daughter Elizabeth died of smallpox in March 1714 she sent the Marlboroughs a letter of condolence, and although the details remain vague, she agreed to reinstate him to his former offices of state. This was actually an indication of another shift in British politics. Robert Harley and Abigail Masham – now a Baroness – had fallen out, and as Harley intrigued, he left himself exposed to criticism, which was duly passed on to the queen. He was dismissed from office as Lord Treasurer in July 1714, just before the Marlboroughs returned to England.

Eventually, Marlborough had to return home. He and his wife had just lost a daughter, and their remaining children needed them. They arrived in Britain on 1 August, only to be met by news that the Queen had died the same day. The German-speaking elector of Hanover was immediately proclaimed King George I of Great Britain, even though he could barely speak a word of English. King George was duly crowned that October, and Marlborough was reinstated to the post of Captain-General, and Master-General of the Ordnance. He was readmitted to court, and King George's first words to the old general were: 'My Lord Duke, I hope your troubles are now over.' Although Marlborough never held another active military command, he had regained all the status and power he had lost three

Work on Blenheim Palace began in 1705, and continued for almost 20 years. Built in the English baroque style by Sir John Vanbrugh, it was less of a stately home than a national monument, paid for from the public purse. (Stratford Archive)

years before. For his part Robert Harley was thrown into the Tower of London, where he faced charges of high treason. Although he was later acquitted, Marlborough's political nemesis was a broken man.

The Duke and Duchess of Marlborough got on with the business of supervising the completion of their vast house – Blenheim Palace – although Sarah disliked its cold, pretentious appearance and unfriendly, sprawling apartments, and they spent most of their time in Marlborough House, their London home on Pall Mall. The Duke and Duchess were now grandparents, and they enjoyed the company of their family, despite the death of their youngest daughter Anne, Countess of Sutherland, in May 1716. Her death may have contributed to Marlborough's first stroke later that month. He had another in November, and this time he lost some of his power of speech. It was clear that his health was fading. Nevertheless, he still managed to travel between London and Blenheim, and he still supervised the building work on his great house.

In early 1719 they were able to move into the completed east wing of Blenheim Palace, and while Sarah continued to dislike the place Marlborough took great satisfaction in watching it near completion. In the end he had only a few years to enjoy the splendours of Blenheim Palace. The Duke of Marlborough suffered another stroke while in Windsor on 15 June 1722, and he slipped into a coma. He died at dawn on 16 June, while his wife and two remaining daughters watched over him. Duchess Sarah said that on his death she felt the soul tearing from her body.

The Duchess organized the funeral, a lavish affair that she insisted would be paid for from her own purse rather than by the state. The cortège wound from Marlborough House to Westminster Abbey, led by the soldiers of the Foot Guards. A carpet of black cloth lined part of the route, and thousands came to pay their last respects. It was a fitting end for the greatest soldier of his age. Sarah outlived her husband by over two decades. Appropriately enough, when she finally died in 1744 she was interred in the chapel at Blenheim, and the body of her husband was moved from Westminster so that he could lie beside her in the palace bequeathed to him by a grateful nation.

A LIFE IN WORDS

John Churchill, Duke of Marlborough, was extremely fortunate in that his most distinguished biographer was one of his most august descendants. Britain's wartime Prime Minister Winston Churchill wrote his masterly biography of his ancestor in the 1930s, shortly before the outbreak of World War II. He said of Marlborough: 'He had consolidated all that England had gained by the revolution of 1688 and the achievements of William III. By his invincible genius in war and his scarcely less admirable qualities of wisdom and management he had completed that glorious process that carried England from her dependency upon France under Charles II to ten years' leadership of Europe.'

Winston Churchill had a way with words, and his eloquent declaration seems to have set the tone for subsequent biographers. Another later and even more distant relative, Charles, Earl Spencer, said of Marlborough: 'It is difficult to understand Marlborough the man. He was enigmatic, focussed, and brilliant. He was also avaricious, and – as we know from his correspondence with the Jacobites – capable of double-dealing. However, his men adored him, and they knew his incomparable military worth: they were proud to point out that he never lost a battle, or failed to take a city that he besieged.'

Winston Churchill was more inclined to dismiss Marlborough's defection to William III, by saying that 'He had proved himself to be the good Englishman he aspired to be', and he continued by adding: 'He was honourable in his public life. He was kind and chivalrous at heart, and in his own home, and to his best beloved. He had a strong, deep faith, which never failed him.' In other words, Churchill was painting his ancestor as the very epitome of the upright English gentleman, doing the right thing, a noble and honourable knight errant.

Certainly, Marlborough was a skilled diplomat, a charming, smooth courtier and a man whose ability to inspire people was notable. In the modern age this would be called 'good people skills'. He also betrayed his king in 1688 and made bad political judgements, which ultimately cost him his military command. He indulged in factional politics and lost, while his wife Sarah made full use of her close association with the Queen to carry on intrigues on his behalf in court. Neither Churchill nor Earl Spencer touch on his political and social failures, and Churchill in particular blames these on his trust in other, less noble characters – political intriguers and self-serving courtiers.

Earl Spencer also raises the important point of Marlborough's continued association with the Jacobites. He maintained a correspondence with the exiled King James, and with other members of the Jacobite court in France, including his cousin James, Duke of Berwick, who was not only a Jacobite but an enemy general – a marshal of France. Before Churchill, historians were less willing to excuse both Marlborough's abandonment of King James and his continued dealings with him. Thomas Macaulay, writing in his *History of England* published in the mid-19th century, saw Marlborough as a man devoid of morals and scruples, who owed his rise to his sister being a mistress, and who was willing to be kept by another 'harlot', Barbara Villers. Macaulay went further, describing him as a traitor for his continued correspondence with the Jacobites, and for aiding the Jacobites by sending them military intelligence. While the latter claim is sheer nonsense, Macaulay was adamant that Marlborough was no gentleman. In other words, his picture of Marlborough was the very reverse of that painted by Churchill almost a century later.

The first historian to question Macaulay's picture was his nephew Sir George Trevelyan, who edited Macaulay's letters in 1876. He argued that his uncle's opinions had been coloured by the political writings of the time, many of which were extremely scurrilous. To Trevelyan, Marlborough had his flaws – his quest for social and political advancement, his financial avarice and his ruthless ambition. However, he argued that Macaulay had gone too far, and had tried to turn Marlborough into a villain. He also admitted that Macaulay was a poet, not a historian. Marlborough – Trevelyan argues – was ruthless, ambitious and greedy, but so too were virtually all other leading figures of the period. Another Victorian author, John Wilson Croker, said of Macaulay that he pursued Marlborough with the ferocity of a bloodhound, and supports Trevelyan's assessment that this was character assassination for the sake of drama, more than a reasoned historical case.

A later historian to follow Macaulay's stance was G. K. Chesterton. In his *Short History of England*, published in 1917, he criticized Marlborough for turning his back on James II, saying: 'Churchill, as if to add something ideal to his imitation of Iscariot, went to James with wanton professions of love and loyalty … and then calmly handed over the army to the invader.' It really comes down to interpretation and bias – Chesterton was a convert to Catholicism, and therefore he saw James' religion as no justification for Marlborough's betrayal. Trevelyan, on the other hand, was a Protestant, and so was more willing to understand Marlborough's claim that he was inspired by his love for the liberties of England and the Protestant religion.

Winston Churchill's *Marlborough: His Life and Times* certainly restored Marlborough's somewhat tarnished reputation, and he admitted that one of the reasons he embarked on the project in the first place was to undo the damage done to Marlborough's name by Macaulay. Today's generation of historians view Marlborough in a favourable light, albeit admitting that he had his faults as a man. David Chandler (1973), Christopher Hibbert (2001), James Falkner (2002) and Richard Holmes (2008) all concentrate on his achievements as a soldier, and most dub him the greatest military commander in British history. This isn't a new view – Marlborough's contemporaries and even his enemies said much the same thing. Even the other soldier who might claim that particular crown – the Duke of Wellington – said: 'I can conceive nothing greater than Marlborough at the head of an English army.' Whatever Marlborough's critics might say, none could detract from the string of victories – Blenheim, Ramillies, Oudenarde and Malplaquet – that demonstrated just how great a military genius Marlborough really was.

BIBLIOGRAPHY

Barnett, Correlli, *Marlborough,* Book Club Associates: London, 1974

Bevan, Bryan, *Marlborough the Man,* Robert Hale Ltd: London, 1975

Chandler, David, *The Art of War in the Age of Marlborough,* Batsford Press: London, 1976

——, *Marlborough as a Military Commander,* Military Book Society: London, 1973

——, *Sedgemoor, 1685: An Account and an Anthology,* Anthony Mott Ltd: London, 1985

—— (ed.), *Military Memoirs of Marlborough's Campaigns, 1702–1712,* Greenhill Books: London, 1988

Childs, John, *The British Army of William III, 1689–1702,* University of Manchester Press: Manchester, 1987

——, *The Nine Years War and the British Army, 1688–97,* University of Manchester Press: Manchester, 1991

——, *The Williamite Wars in Ireland, 1688–1691,* Hambledon Continuum: London, 2007

Churchill, Winston S., *Marlborough: His Life and Times,* (six volumes), Ballantyne Press: London, 1938

Corvisier, André, *La Bataille de Malplaquet, 1709,* Economica: Paris, 1997

Duffy, Christopher, *Siege Warfare: Fortress in the Age of Vauban and Frederick the Great, 1660–1789,* Routledge: London, 1985

Falkner, James, *Great and Glorious Days: Marlborough's Battles, 1704–09,* Spellmount: Staplehurst, Kent, 2002

——, *Blenheim, 1704: Marlborough's Greatest Victory,* Leo Cooper: Barnsley, Yorkshire, 2004

——, *Marlborough Goes to War: Eyewitness Accounts, 1702–1713,* Leo Cooper: Barnsley, Yorkshire, 2005

——, *Marlborough's Sieges,* The History Press: Stroud, Gloucestershire, 2006

——, *Ramillies, 1706: Year of Miracles,* Pen & Sword: Barnsley, Yorkshire, 2006

——, *James Falkner's Guide to Marlborough's Battlefields,* Pen & Sword: Barnsley, Yorkshire, 2008

Field, Ophelia, *The Favourite: Sarah, Duchess of Marlborough,* Hodder & Stoughton: London, 2002

Fleming, Kate: *The Churchills,* Penguin [Viking]: London, 1975

Grant, Charles S., *From Pike to Shot*: *Armies and Battles in Western Europe, 1685 to 1720,* Wargames Research Group: Camberley, Surrey, 1986

——, *The Armies of the Duke of Marlborough's Wars,* Partizan Press: Leigh-on-Sea, 2004

Gregg, Edward, *Queen Anne,* Routledge & Kegan Paul: London, 1980

Haythornthwaite, Philip J., *Invincible Generals,* Firebird Books: Poole, Dorset, 1991

Hibbert, Christopher, *The Marlboroughs: John and Sarah Churchill, 1650–1744,* Penguin [Viking]: London, 2001

Hussey, John, *John Churchill, Duke of Marlborough: Hero of Blenheim,* Weidenfeld & Nicholson: London, 2004

Holmes, Richard, *Marlborough: England's Fragile Genius,* Harper Press: London, 2008

Kearsey, A., *Marlborough and his Campaigns,* Gale & Polden: Aldershot, Surrey, 1958

Litten, Neil, *Ramillies: Marlborough's Masterpiece,* Partizan Press: Leigh-on-Sea, Essex, 2007

Lynn, John A., *The Wars of Louis XIV, 1667–1714,* Addison Wesley Longman: Harlow, Essex, 1999

Nosworthy, Brent, *The Anatomy of Victory: Battle Tactics, 1689–1763,* Hippocrene: New York, 1992

Ostwald, Jamel, *Vauban Under Siege: Engineering Efficiency and Martial Vigour in the War of the Spanish Succession,* Brill: Boston, 2007

Scott, Christopher, *The Battle of Oudenarde, 1708,* Partizan Press: Leigh-on-Sea, 2007

——, *Malplaquet, 1709* Partizan Press: Nottingham, 2009

Scouller, Raibeart Elder, *The Armies of Queen Anne,* Clarendon Press: Oxford, 1966

Spencer, Charles, *Blenheim: Battle for Europe,* Phoenix: London, 2005

Stanford, Iain, *Marlborough goes to War: The Campaign and Battle of Blenheim, 1704,* Pike & Shot Society: Farnham, Surrey, 2002

Thomson, George Malcolm, *The First Churchill: the Life of John, 1st Duke of Marlborough,* Secker & Warburg: London, 1979

Tincey, John, *Blenheim, 1704: The Duke of Marlborough's Masterpiece,* Osprey Publishing: Oxford, 2004

——, *Sedgemoor, 1685: Marlborough's First Victory,* Pen & Sword: Barnsley, Yorkshire, 2005

Watson, J. N. P., *Marlborough's Shadow: The Life of the First Earl Cadogan,* Leo Cooper: Barnsley, Yorkshire, 2002

INDEX